Simple Pre-diabetes Action Plan Cookbook For Beginners

Aidene .J Hille

I probably use my chef's knives more than any other tool in the kitchen. I'm not married to a particular brand, because they all work, they all have sharp blades. - Bobby Flay

I'm not a chef. But I'm passionate about food - the tradition of it, cooking it, and sharing it. - Zac Posen

I was a hostess, a waitress, a cafe manager, and a prep chef. For one job, I had to wear a hat shaped like a head of garlic. - Jenna Blum

A chef and a restaurateur are different jobs: One is about pleasing people with what's on the plate; the other is about understanding the market. I'm a chef, but I think I'm a savvy businessperson, too. - Jean-Georges Vongerichten

Being a great baker and pastry chef requires the upmost open mind. I try every dessert that comes my way! - Christina Tosi

How diet relates to prediabetes

Many factors can increase your risk of developing prediabetes.

Genetics can play a role, especially if diabetes runs in your family. However, other factors play a larger role in the development of prediabetes. Not getting enough physical activity and having overweight are other potential risk factors.

In prediabetes, sugar from food begins to build up in your bloodstream because insulin can't easily move the sugar into your cells.

The amount and type of carbohydrates you consume at a meal influence your blood sugar. A diet filled with refined and processed carbohydrates that digest quickly can cause higher spikes in blood sugar.

If you have prediabetes, your body likely has a difficult time lowering your blood sugar levels after meals. Watching your carb intake can help you avoid blood sugar spikes.

1. Eat more fiber-rich foods

Fiber offers several benefits. It helps you feel full longer. It also adds bulk to your diet, making bowel movements easier to pass.

Eating fiber-rich foods can make you less likely to

overeat and help you avoid the "crash" that can come from eating a high sugar food. High sugar foods will often give you a big boost of energy but make you feel tired shortly afterward.

Examples of high fiber foods include:

beans and legumes
fruits and vegetables that have an edible skin
whole grains such as quinoa and barley
whole grain breads
whole grain cereals
whole wheat pasta

2. Watch your carb intake

The glycemic index (GI) is a tool you can use to determine how a particular food could affect your blood sugar.

In general, foods that have a high GI will raise your blood sugar faster. Foods with a lower GI have less of an effect on your blood sugar.

However, different people's bodies may process these foods differently. Additionally, cooking a food or eating it along with protein or fat can change its GI.

It's also important to be mindful of portion sizes. Eating a large amount of any carbohydrate-containing food can cause your blood sugar levels to rise.

Low GI foods
Foods that have a low GI, such as high fiber foods, are best for your blood sugar.

Incorporate the following items into your diet:

steel cut oats, as opposed to instant oatmeal
stone-ground whole wheat bread
pasta, preferably whole wheat
non-starchy vegetables such as carrots and leafy greens
beans
sweet potatoes
nuts and seeds
Food and nutrition labels don't mention the GI of a given food. Instead, take note of the fiber content listed on the label in order to determine a food's GI ranking.

Medium GI foods
Foods that rank in the medium range on the GI are fine to eat if you have prediabetes, although it's important to keep portions to about 1/2 cupTrusted Source. Examples include whole wheat bread, brown rice, and corn.

High GI foods
Foods that are refined, processed, and lacking in fiber and other nutrients register high on the GI scale.

Refined carbohydrates are one example. These are

products, mostly grains or sugars, that digest quickly in your stomach. Some examples are:

white bread
russet potatoes — although eating the skin may lower the GI
sugar-sweetened soda
juice
If you have prediabetes, it's important to limit these foods and drinks.

Eating mixed meals is a great way to lower a food's GI. For example, if you plan to eat white rice, adding vegetables and chicken cooked in a small amount of healthy fat can slow down the digestion of the grain and minimize blood sugar spikes.

3. Be mindful of portion sizes

Paying attention to portion sizes can help you keep your diet low on the GI scale.

Often, portions sizes in the United States are much larger than intended serving sizes. Food labels can help you determine how much you're actually eating. The label will list calories, fat, carbohydrates, and other nutrition information for a particular serving.

If you eat more than the serving listed, it's important to understand how that will affect the nutritional value. A food may have 20 grams of carbohydrates and 150 calories per serving. If you have 2 servings, you'll consume 40 grams of carbohydrates and 300 calories.

However, it's not necessary to eliminate carbohydrates entirely.

A large 2018 studyTrusted Source in more than 15,000 adults showed that a lower carb diet (less than 40% carbs) is associated with the same mortality risk increase as a high carb diet (more than 70% carbs) in adults.

The study noted minimal risk observed when people consumed a moderate amount of carbohydrates (50% to 55% carbs in a day). On a 1,600-calorie diet, this would equal 200 to 220 grams of carbohydrates daily.

This is in line with the Dietary Guidelines for Americans' recommendation to consume 45% to 65%Trusted Source of daily calories from carbohydrates. Spreading intake evenly throughout the day is best.

Carbohydrate needs vary based on your stature and activity level. It's a good idea to consult a registered dietitian to discuss your specific needs.

One of the best ways to manage portions is to practice mindful eating. Eat when you're hungry. Stop when you're full. Sit while you eat, and eat slowly. Focus on the food and flavors.

DID YOU KNOW?
When you eat more calories than your body needs, the calories get stored as fat. This can cause you to gain weight.

Body fat, especially around the belly, is linkedTrusted Source to insulin resistance. This explains why many people with prediabetes also have overweight.

4. Eat lean meats and other proteins

Meat doesn't contain carbohydrates, but it can be a significant source of fat in your diet. Eating a lot of unhealthy fats can lead to prediabetes as well as high cholesterol and heart disease.

If you have prediabetes, eating a diet low in saturated fat and trans fat can help reduce your risk of developing heart disease.

Choose protein sources such as the following:

beans and legumes
soybean products, such as tofu and tempeh
low fat Greek yogurt
eggs
chicken
turkey
fish, such as cod, flounder, haddock, halibut, tuna,

and trout

shellfish, such as crab, lobster, shrimp, and scallops

lean beef cuts, such as flank steak, ground round, tenderloin, and roast with the fat trimmed

Cooking chicken or turkey with the skin on will preserve moisture and have little effect on the fat content. However, the skin should be removed before eating.

Avoid cuts of meat, such as beef, that have visible fat or skin.

5. Drink alcohol in moderation

Moderation is a healthy rule to live by in most instances. Drinking alcohol is no exception.

Many alcoholic beverages are dehydrating. In addition, some cocktails may contain high amounts of sugar, which can cause blood sugar spikes.

According to the Dietary Guidelines for AmericansTrusted Source, women should have only one drink per day and men should have no more than two drinks per day.

The following are the measurements for an average single drink:

1 bottle of beer = 12 fluid ounces (fl. oz.)
1 glass of wine = 5 fl. oz.

1 shot of distilled spirits, such as gin, vodka, or whiskey = 1.5 fl. oz.

Keep your drink as simple as possible and avoid adding sugary juices or liqueurs.

Also, keep a glass of water nearby that you can sip on to prevent dehydration.

6. Drink plenty of water

Water is an important part of any healthy diet. It's essential to drink enough water each day to keep yourself from becoming dehydrated.

If you have prediabetes, water is a healthier option than sugary sodas, juices, or energy drinks. These beverages typically contain calories that translate to quick-digesting carbohydrates and have little or no other nutritional value.

A single 12-ounce can of regular soda may contain around 40 grams of carbohydrates. Water is a better choice to quench your thirst.

The amount of water you should drink every day depends on your body size, your activity level, and the climate you live in.

You can determine whether you're drinking enough water by monitoring the volume of urine when you go. Take note of the color as well. Your urine should be pale yellow.

7. Remember that exercise and diet go together

Exercise is a part of any healthy lifestyle. It's especially important if you have prediabetes.

A lack of physical activity has been linked to increased insulin resistance, according to the National Institute of Diabetes and Digestive and Kidney DiseasesTrusted Source. Exercise causes muscles to use glucose (sugar) for energy and makes the cells work more effectively with insulin.

The Physical Activity Guidelines for AmericansTrusted Source recommend that adults get at least:

150 to 300 minutes of moderate-intensity aerobic activity per week or
75 to 150 minutes of vigorous-intensity aerobic activity per week or
an equivalent combination of moderate- and vigorous-intensity aerobic activity each week
Exercise doesn't have to be overly complicated. Consider walking, dancing, riding a bicycle, or any other physical activity you enjoy.

Recent guidelines, such as the American Diabetes Association (ADA) Standards of Care, also emphasize the importance of physical activity for people with prediabetes or diabetes. An active lifestyle may prevent a person with prediabetes from developing type 2 diabetes and help a person with diabetes manage their blood sugar levels.

One of the ADA's recommendations states that adults should avoid sitting for more than 30 minutes at a time. You may want to try breaking up your sitting time by doing a few squats, toe raises, or knee raises.

The takeaway
The Centers for Disease Control and PreventionTrusted Source estimates that 96 million U.S. adults have prediabetes. Perhaps even more concerning is that more than 80% don't know they have the condition.

Early medical intervention is important to identify the condition before it develops into type 2 diabetes. If you've received a diagnosis of prediabetes, you and your doctor can develop a diet plan that will help.

Table of content

Blueberry-Chia Smoothie
Cherry, Chocolate, and Almond Shake
Stovetop Granola
Seedy Muesli
Overnight Oats
Apple Millet Porridge
Breakfast Banana Barley
Harvest Blackberry Quinoa Bowl
High-Protein Oatmeal
Carrot Cake Oatmeal
Strawberry-Ricotta Toast
Easy Buckwheat Crêpes
Shakshuka
Eggplant Breakfast Sandwich
Perfect Egg Scramble with Simple Salad
Avocado-Tofu Scramble with Roasted Potatoes

Citrus Avocado Salad
Herbed Tomato Salad
Spinach Salad with Strawberries and Toasted
Almonds
Asparagus Salad with Chile-Lime Dressing
Kale Caesar Salad
Pomegranate "Tabbouleh" with Cauliflower

CHAPTER ONE

Living with Prediabetes

Prediabetes is a serious global health concern. More than one in three American adults have prediabetes, and, according to the Centers for Disease Control and Prevention, up to 90 percent are unaware of their condition.

According to the American Diabetes Association, prediabetes may be reversible through the implementation of lifestyle changes, which include a healthier diet and increased exercise. It is challenging, however, to take the necessary steps while your busy schedule and the demands of daily life command so much time and attention. This time issue is the main reason I have limited the recipes to 30 minutes (or less): to help limit stress while maintaining nutritional balance.

In this chapter, you will learn more about prediabetes and how it differs from the diagnosis of diabetes. You will also become familiar with the current medical treatments of prediabetes through diet, medication, physical activity, and other ways to lower your risk in regard to developing into the next stage.

Understanding Prediabetes

Prediabetes is a chronic metabolic condition that occurs when blood glucose levels rise higher than normal, but below the threshold for diabetes. Diagnosing prediabetes is based on laboratory values from more than one test and includes the following blood sugar measurements: fasting plasma glucose (FPG), impaired glucose tolerance (IGT—during the oral glucose tolerance test [OGTT]), and A1C or average blood glucose level. The IFG (impaired fasting glucose) and IGT show your blood glucose levels at the time you test your blood, and the A1C reflects your average blood glucose over the past 60 to 90 days.

	Normal	Prediabetes	Diabetes
FPG	<100 mg/dL	100–125 mg/dL	≥126 mg/dL
IGT	<140 mg/dL	140–199 mg/dL	≥200 mg/dL
A1C	<5.7%	5.7–6.4%	≥6.5%

Typically, prediabetes occurs in those who have some insulin resistance, which is when beta cells on the pancreas do not make enough insulin to keep blood glucose within a normal range. Insulin is an essential hormone in the body because without it, glucose stays in your blood and does not enter your cells. Think of insulin as a key. Glucose from the blood needs this key to unlock and enter the cell walls so that the cells can use the glucose as energy to deliver oxygen throughout your body.

The Causes of Prediabetes

Prediabetes can be caused by various factors—many of which you cannot control. These uncontrollable factors are termed "non-modifiable risk factors." Other risk factors, however, you can regulate. Modifiable risk factors may require the use of medications, and others may take changing behaviors.

Modifiable Risk Factors:

- High blood pressure

- High levels of triglycerides

- Inactivity

- Low levels of high-density lipoprotein (HDL), the "good" cholesterol

- Excess weight or obesity

- Poor or inadequate diet

Non-Modifiable Risk Factors:

- Age 45 or older

- Ethnicity: Although it is unclear why, people of certain races—including African American, Alaska Native, South Asian, American Indian,

Latino/Hispanic, Native Hawaiian, or Pacific Islander American—are more likely to develop prediabetes.

- Family history with type 2 diabetes from a parent, brother, or sister

- Gestational diabetes, which is diabetes during pregnancy, can affect both the mother and the child

- Personal history of heart disease or stroke

- Personal history of polycystic ovary syndrome (PCOS), a common condition characterized by irregular menstrual periods, excess hair growth, and obesity

Also, there are risk factors that may contribute to insulin resistance; these include:

- Cushing's syndrome, acromegaly, and other hormonal disorders

- Excess abdominal weight—the weight that accumulates around your midsection

- Medications like glucocorticoids, some types of HIV medications, and antipsychotics

- Obstructive sleep apnea or other sleep problems

- Tobacco smoke

If you are overweight or obese and have one or more of the other aforementioned risk factors for diabetes, you should be tested for prediabetes. If results are normal and you have other risk factors, you should retest at a minimum of every three years. The sooner you get tested, the sooner you can act to improve your health and, thus, the better your outcome will be in the long run.

How Prediabetes Can Affect You

Blood sugar levels are often not high enough to cause chronic symptoms for most individuals. However, there is evidence that suggests some people with prediabetes may have early changes in their eyes, which can eventually lead to retinopathy. Retinopathy is damage to any part of the retina, which can cause blurry vision and permanent damage to your eyes. Blood vessels that lead to the eyes are microscopic, and when cells do not get the oxygen they need, the eyes become affected in many ways that can eventually lead to blindness.

In addition to the effect on the eyes, those who are prediabetic are at risk for developing type 2 diabetes. Even if you do not develop type 2 diabetes, prediabetes is also linked to cardiovascular disease and kidney damage because of the increased strain on the heart and demand on the kidneys.

Along with the effects on your body, prediabetes can also have major implications on your mental and emotional state. Sudden mood changes may occur, including nervousness, sadness, difficulty thinking, anger or anxiety, and feeling tired (low energy). These sudden changes and negative feelings are caused by an increase in blood sugar levels that influence emotional response and can cause emotional strain on all aspects of your personal life and relationships. A recent study from Wolf et al. at Iowa State University found that "People with type 2 diabetes and prediabetes were more likely to focus on and have a strong emotional response to threats and negative things, which affects quality of life and increases risk for depression."

While prediabetes is increasingly common, it's more important to note that it is reversible. This book can help anyone living with prediabetes (and diabetes) by aiding with the simple, proven lifestyle change known as "your diet."

What to Know About the Types of Diabetes

Diabetes refers specifically to having high blood glucose. The causes of the higher levels of glucose varies, which is why there are different types of diabetes. The main and most talked-about types are type 1, type 2, and gestational diabetes (often abbreviated to GDM).

Type 1 | This form of diabetes is usually diagnosed in youth, but it can develop at any age and in people of every race, shape, and size. Type 1 diabetics either do not make insulin in their pancreas, or the insulin produced is not enough. This shortfall of insulin is caused by the immune system mistakenly attacking the cells that make insulin. It is less common than type 2 diabetes, and treatment options are limited to insulin injections. With nearly one-fifth of the population afraid of needles, this can be anxiety-inducing, especially when a child is told to take insulin injections for life. Carbohydrate counting is necessary, as well as understanding the effects of exercise and how to create a balance among these factors.

Type 2 | The most common form of diabetes is type 2. It's progressive and multifactorial. Insulin resistance and increased glucose production from the liver are hallmark features. When these factors are combined, more insulin is required to be released, but it cannot keep up with the high glucose levels. Over time, the cells that release the insulin cannot be maintained and lose their function, resulting in cell death and insulin deficiency. Heredity plays a key role in the presence of type 2 diabetes; however, it is the environmental influences that turn genes on or off. These are the previously discussed modifiable risk factors, including exposure to chemicals and medications.

Gestational | GDM is associated with insulin resistance due to pregnancy, possibly obesity, and genetics. It is also associated with an increased risk of diabetes for the mother after the birth. Maternal risks include cesarean delivery, hypertension, and polyhydramnios (an increase in amniotic fluid), which in turn increases the risk of morbidity and mortality. After delivery, blood sugars typically return to normal, but should continue to be checked 6 to 12 weeks postpartum.

Current Treatments

The aforementioned diagnostic criteria from two laboratory values guide the treatment options available for people with diabetes. The landmark Diabetes Prevention Program (DPP) was a study on more than 14,000 high-risk people for prediabetes. This study demonstrated that interventions with intensive lifestyle modifications like improved eating, physical activity, and weight loss reduced incidence by 58 percent versus those who used medication intervention (metformin) that reduced their weight by 31 percent. A 10-year follow-up to the DPP study showed a reduction of diabetes by 34 percent in the lifestyle group versus 18 percent in the medication group.

More doctors are testing for prediabetes and diabetes with increased awareness, knowing the importance of early detection for immediate attention. Depending on the individual and their medical history, the treatment strategy should be tailored specifically to that person. Regardless of the treatment, it is well-advised for each individual, including family members and caretakers, to receive additional diabetes education. Consult a certified diabetes educator (CDE—recently changed to certified diabetes care and education specialist [CDCES]) and nutrition education from a registered dietitian.

Diet Modification

Optimizing nutrition through a person's diet is the underlying principle of prediabetes lifestyle change recommendations. Choosing nutrient-dense, high-fiber foods in moderation instead of heavily processed foods with added sugar, fat, and sodium is a must. And let us not forget the addictive sugar-sweetened beverages that are a major culprit of increased blood sugars—cut soda out of your diet today. Every other type of food can be included in a healthy diet. It's about creating balance and choosing healthier foods such as lean protein sources and unsaturated fats, while drinking plenty of water and eating three to five servings of vegetables throughout the day.

When you start restricting food choices and using negative language when talking about food, it hurts your relationship with food. It is for this reason why this book uses ingredients that often get a bad rap, such as honey. When consumed in excess, honey can be harmful to your health, but when eaten in moderation within a balanced meal, honey can provide health benefits.

Another example is the ingestion of carbohydrates. It's a common myth that carbs are bad for you. They're not. Carbohydrates are the preferred source of fuel for the body, more specifically the brain and central nervous system. Some carbs are healthier than others, such as whole-grain, complex, and high-fiber foods. People view carbs negatively, but it's important not to forget the benefits they provide for your heart and that they keep you fuller longer (a double bonus!).

Creating a balance in macronutrients (carbohydrates, proteins, and fats) at each meal is fundamental, with an overall goal of weight loss using lifestyle modification. Think of weight loss as 80 percent eating and 20 percent exercise.

Medications

Although lifestyle changes are the focus when it comes to prediabetes, medications may be recommended as well. Metformin therapy is most commonly prescribed and should be considered for prediabetics with body mass index (BMI) ≥35kg/m^2, those under 60 years of age, and women with prior GDM. Metformin improves blood glucose control by decreasing the amount of glucose the liver makes, decreasing the amount of glucose absorbed by the intestines, and improving insulin sensitivity.

People with prediabetes have a higher risk for cardiovascular disease (CVD). Prioritizing and treating CVD risk factors is crucial; therefore, equal emphasis must be given to hypertension and dyslipidemia. This is the reason why medications for these conditions may be warranted. A person's laboratory values, previous medical history, and anthropometrics such as waist circumference, weight, and BMI are used to determine treatment options and goals.

The number of cholesterol-lowering medications is vast. They are grouped into six drug classes, but the most recommended belong to statins, the only cholesterol-lowering drug class with a direct association in risk reduction of a heart attack or stroke.

You should have a 10-year risk assessment from your doctor to determine your need for cholesterol-lowering medications. They will weigh the pros and cons of medication therapy. Perhaps medications are not required and lifestyle changes alone may be all you need! This is why I am providing these easy, quick recipes to help with the diet component.

Embracing Exercise

In addition to diet, it's essential to address your activity level when discussing risk reduction of prediabetes, diabetes, and living a healthier life. Recommendations are to get at least 150 minutes of exercise each week, or roughly 30 minutes at least five days a week.

Hopefully this doesn't send your jaw dropping to the floor, because this is only a suggestion. Everyone has their limitations, and it's always best to start slowly and gradually. If you don't exercise at all, this may seem impossible. The key is to choose something you love to do that gets your body moving. Maybe it's a brisk walk around the neighborhood, doing chair exercises in your home, or doing something completely new like snowshoeing. Bring a friend for support if that helps you stay on track.

You do not have to hit the gym and spend your money on expensive gym equipment or workout classes. Getting in a home workout is just as effective and can save you money. Using soup cans as weights or even your own body weight is a great place to start. Perhaps you start out doing 10 minutes of stretching in the morning and later in the day take a walk on your lunch break. Every minute counts!

In a society in which our time is of the essence, you may have the excuse of "There just isn't enough time to exercise and cook a nutritious meal." This book will give you the free time to put toward your workout. Many of the recipes can be made in advance or multiplied to save you even more precious time.

Dietary Herbs and Supplements: Are They Worth It?

Nontraditional treatments consisting of dietary herbs and supplements are commonly used because these products often make promising claims. They do not require proof of safety, effectiveness, and purity, which is why you must be cautious and should consult with a registered dietitian and doctor before deciding to take supplements. Side effects and drug interactions are a high possibility.

Many of the products listed in the following chart have real effects that eventually may prove to be beneficial. However, at this point, these products lack the high-quality evidence of safety and effectiveness needed to recommend them for long-term use.

If supplements are something you take or are considering, make sure they are tested by a third party, like ConsumerLab.com, NSF International, or the US Pharmacopeia (USP). These organizations provide evaluations of supplements to help you decide which brands are reliable. They test the supplement ingredients for identity, strength, quality, and purity.

Above all, be sure to discuss the benefits and risks of any supplements or herbs with your doctor.

* These proposed recommendations are based solely on the Safety and

Recommendation Chart for Natural Medicines Used for Diabetes

EFFECTIVENESS	SAFETY			
	LIKELY SAFE	POSSIBLY SAFE	INSUFFICIENT EVIDENCE	POSSIBLY UNSAFE
LIKELY EFFECTIVE				
POSSIBLY EFFECTIVE	American ginseng Blond psyllium Cassia cinnamon Flaxseed Magnesium Oats Soy Xanthan gum	Aloe Alpha-lipoic acid Banaba Chromium Fenugreek Glucomannan Guarumo Inulin Ivy gourd Prickly pear cactus Siberian ginseng White mulberry		
INSUFFICIENT EVIDENCE	Coenzyme Q10 Stevia Vanadium	Bitter melon Chia Gymnema Asian ginseng		

		Common bean			
POSSIBLY INEFFECTIVE	Flaxseed oil				Selenium

Consider this product

Don't recommend using this product

Recommend against using this product

Chart is modified from the Natural Medicines Database.

Talk to Your Doctor

Upon diagnosis, talk to your doctor to address any concerns you may have. They will guide you through key management strategies, answer your questions, and follow up with you on a regular basis to keep you on track to prevent diabetes from occurring. It is generally recommended to visit with your health provider at least every six months and more frequently if needed once diagnosed with prediabetes. As mentioned earlier, working with a certified diabetes educator and registered dietitian as well as your primary care provider can be instrumental in your journey to making lifestyle changes. They can help you stay on track with your health goals and provide counsel.

Consider asking these questions:

1. Why do I need to know about managing my blood sugars?

2. What are the symptoms of prediabetes?

3. What can I do to delay or prevent type 2 diabetes?

4. What are my risk factors for developing type 2 diabetes?

5. Are there support groups I can attend?

6. What lifestyle changes can I make to reduce my risk of prediabetes or d

7. What, if any, medications would you recommend I take to prevent type diabetes, including those related to blood pressure and cholesterol?

8. Is there a National Diabetes Prevention Program organization I can joi local?

9. How is my diet influencing my blood sugars?

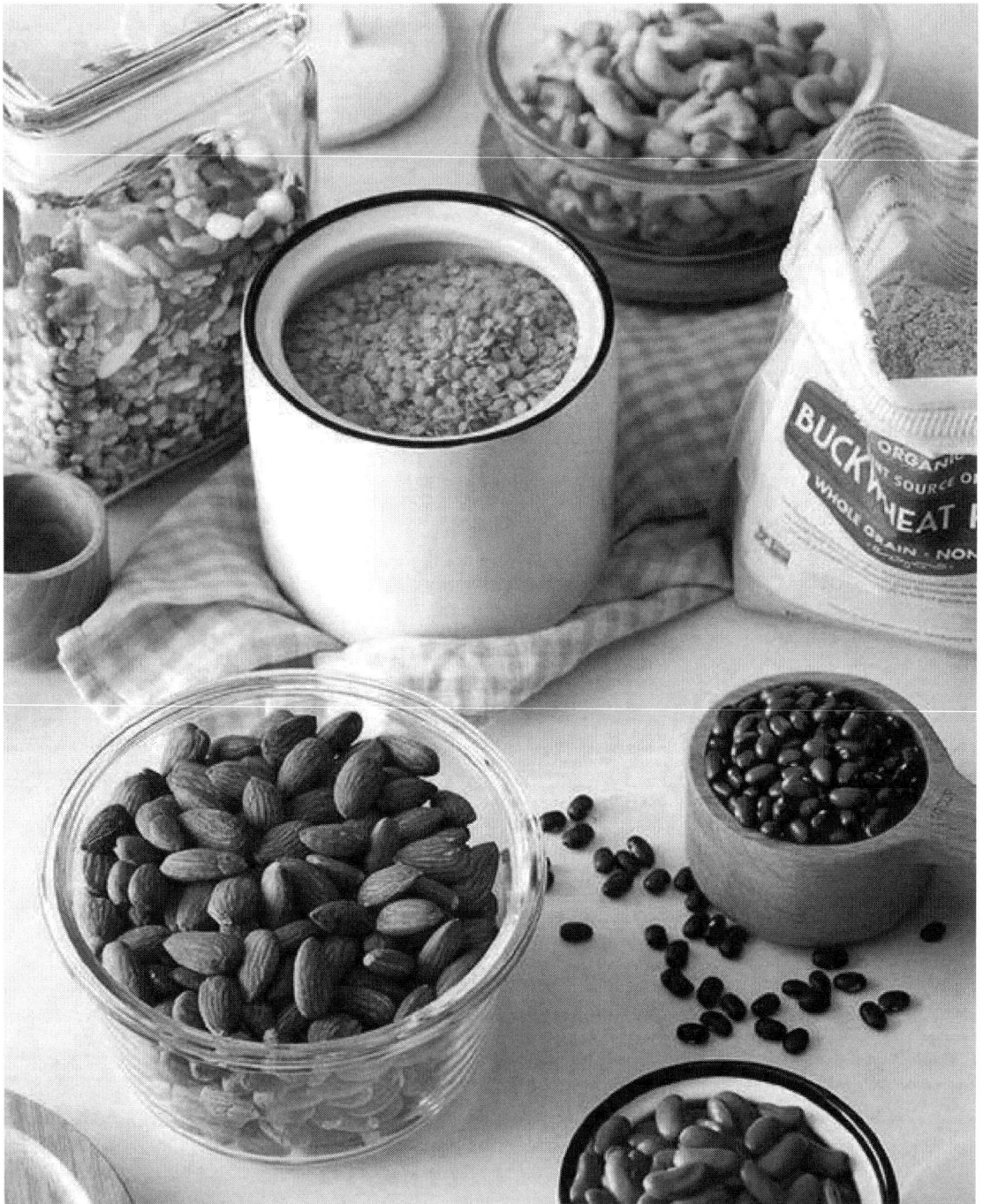

CHAPTER TWO

Eating to Manage Your Prediabetes

What you feed your body affects all aspects of your health, as well as your current and future state of being. It's important to remember that you may not be able to tell if someone is healthy only by looking at them—people come in all shapes and sizes. The decisions you make about what you eat can have extreme consequences for your body over time, especially if you have prediabetes or a chronic disease like diabetes. Read on to learn more and to understand how your diet specifically affects your health and well-being.

The Link between Food and Prediabetes

Your diet plays an incredibly important role in regulating health and wellness, affecting the potential for developing significant diseases like diabetes. Food is made up of protein, fat, and carbohydrates and acts as fuel for the body, keeping it functioning properly. While you may not always see how food affects the body, at a metabolic level the foods you choose to eat impact everything from stress to sleep to energy levels and mood.

The key source of fuel for your body comes from the carbohydrates found in food. These are separated into three main groups: starch, sugar, and fiber. Carbs are not popular in many diets lately, but they remain essential to your health. Some are healthier than others, as they take longer to process in the body and keep you full for longer: Whole-grains, whole fruits, beans, and vegetables are all excellent sources of carbohydrates. Less desirable are simpler carbs, which get used for energy quickly—these include white bread, white rice, juice, soda, and candy. When we consume these simple carbohydrate foods in excess, our bodies have difficulty naturally controlling our blood sugars. Foods with starch and sugar get broken down into glucose, but over time an excess of glucose builds in our blood, and that can lead to prediabetes and diabetes. Couple this with inadequate sleep and water consumption, increased stress, poor diet, and a lack of exercise (among other risk factors), and the risk for diabetes increases.

Sugar and the Glycemic Index

Sugar is one of the main types of carbohydrates found in foods, which provide your body with energy. Let's take it even further to distinguish between naturally occurring sugars and added sugars. The sugars found in milk and fruit are naturally occurring examples. The sugar found in processed foods, like the syrup in canned fruit or baked goods like cookies, was added during preparation. Foods with added sugars have a higher impact on your blood sugars, as they are processed much more quickly in the body.

The best ways to watch sugar levels include:

* serving yourself smaller portions and making your own food at home

* avoiding "flavored" products such as strawberry yogurt (add fresh strawberries to plain yogurt instead)

* swapping out soda for water

* eating more protein and fat

* checking food labels for sugar amounts, as packaging can sometimes be misleading

* focusing on whole foods with no sugar added

A glycemic index (GI) is used to help understand the impact of food on blood sugar. More specifically, a GI provides a value for foods, which gives us an idea of exactly *how* quickly (or slowly) these foods cause your blood sugar levels to increase. Foods with a lower GI, such as beans and milk, tend to release glucose slowly and steadily, while higher GI foods, such as potatoes, white bread, and white rice, release glucose rapidly.

The reason GI can be a beneficial tool for those with prediabetes and diabetes is that it acts as a guide for healthy decision-making. The GI is not the only benchmark to use when considering food; the total amount of carbohydrates and overall nutritional quality is important as well. Those with prediabetes or diabetes, or at risk, can choose foods with a lower GI to nurture weight loss and provide better blood glucose control. On the other hand, high GI foods play an important role in energy recovery after a workout and can help offset low blood sugars.

Understanding Carbohydrates

A common myth about those with prediabetes or diabetes is that they must avoid carbohydrates. The fact remains, carbohydrates are essential to the body, providing the bulk of its fuel. Rather than avoiding carbohydrates, the key is to understand how to eat them in moderation to keep blood sugars in check, while focusing on eating more of the healthier types of carbohydrates.

Another way to think about carbohydrates is based on their chemical structure, notably those that are simple (sometimes called simple sugars) or complex (starch). The most significant difference between the two is how quickly the body digests and absorbs each.

Simple carbohydrates are found in natural foods like fruit, milk, and some vegetables, but they are also found in many processed foods. These types of carbohydrates break down rather quickly and, when eaten in excess, can spike blood sugars.

Structurally, complex carbohydrates are made up of long chains of sugars that require a longer time for the body to break down. Whole-grain foods and starchy vegetables are the bulk of these foods, but there are also refined starches that are technically complex, such as cakes, pastries, and white bread. When dietitians advise "eating more complex," they are referring to whole-grain foods and starchy vegetables because of their slower absorption, keeping you fuller for longer. Refined carbohydrates lack the fiber that is found in whole grains because of the processing the food undergoes. In fact, refined carbs can sometimes raise blood glucose levels as quickly as simple sugars.

Cholesterol, the Good (and the Bad) Kind

Cholesterol is an essential waxy substance found in many foods and within our cells. It is used to make hormones and vitamin D and in the digestive process. Two main types of cholesterol, the "good" and the "bad," seem to be mentioned frequently, but there is also another primary type called very low-density lipoprotein (VLDL) that promotes plaque buildup.

How do you know which cholesterol is good or bad?

"Good" refers to high-density lipoprotein or HDL. Think of the "H" as a helper, because it helps remove excess cholesterol in your blood and transport it back to your liver, where it is broken down and removed from the body. Examples of foods that help increase your HDL are whole grains and plants with high fiber, fish, and plant-based fats such as extra-virgin olive oil, avocado, flax, and chia seeds.

"Bad" refers to low-density lipoprotein or LDL. You can remember this by associating the "L" with the word "lousy." LDL can lead to a buildup of plaque in the arteries and narrowing of the passageways. Sometimes a clot can develop and get stuck, causing a heart attack or stroke. It is for these reasons that you should limit the foods that increase your LDL cholesterol: beef, lamb, poultry, pork, butter, cream, coconut, and palm oil.

The Seven Self-Care Behaviors

Diabetes care and education specialists developed seven key areas for those diagnosed with prediabetes or diabetes. The ADCES (Association of Diabetes Care & Education Specialists) uses a framework called the "Seven Self-Care Behaviors." These behaviors are essential for successful and effective diabetes self-management outcomes.

1. Healthy eating: Having diabetes doesn't mean you can't enjoy the foods you love, but you need to know how food affects your blood sugars. Learn how your current diet affects your health and which gradual changes to make for positive impact.

2. Being active: It's not only about weight loss. Being active can help lower cholesterol, improve blood pressure, lower stress/anxiety, lower blood sugars, and improve your mood.

3. Monitoring: When you test your blood sugars at different times, before and after activity, and before and after eating, you will see how your lifestyle affects your blood sugars. Regular checks mean you can take action sooner and improve your sugars faster.

4. Taking medication: It's essential to take your medications as prescribed and know how they work. There are several that are often recommended and required due to the complexity of managing health during diabetes.

5. Problem solving: Learning how to problem-solve is important for managing prediabetes and diabetes. There's no one-size-fits-all approach to diabetes, so it's important to figure out what works best for you.

6. Healthy coping: Both your emotions and body can be affected by diabetes; it's natural. Coping means taking steps to lower the negative impact your emotions may have on your self-care.

7. Reducing risks: Having diabetes puts you at a higher risk of developing other serious health conditions. It's important to know what they are and how you can reduce them.

A New Approach to Food

Food is exciting, and I'm going to prove that with the recipes in this book. I challenge you to try something new and look at food differently. You don't have to make dramatic changes to your diet and avoid the foods you love. It's all about moderation and fitting in the foods you love with a focus on plant-based choices. There are countless culinary variations in this book that you likely haven't tried or eaten before now. That can be intimidating if you are in a food rut.

How do I recommend breaking out of that rut? Start with one new food. Cook it several different ways: roast, sauté, bake, stuff, steam, and more. You'll likely enjoy eating the new food in one of these preparations. If you try something 8 to 10 times, odds are you will grow to like it. How amazing! You can train your palate to enjoy nutritious foods, but you don't have to do it alone. The entire family can benefit, so do this together. Your heart, mind, body, and spirit will thank you for it.

Foods to Embrace

Eat to feel good by making sure you are getting plenty of whole fruits, vegetables, and grains; lean meats; plant-based protein, like unsalted nuts and seeds; and less added sugar and processed foods. You may recognize that some of these foods contain carbohydrates—these are the healthier sources. They should not be avoided.

Common diabetes superfoods are those rich in vitamins, minerals, antioxidants, and fiber, including:

Beans are high in fiber, magnesium, and potassium.

Berries are packed with antioxidants, vitamins such as vitamin K and C, manganese, potassium, and fiber. They are perfect for those sweet cravings you may encounter.

Dairy products like milk and yogurt are rich in vitamin D and calcium. Look for plain yogurt instead of flavored, and if you want more bang for your nutrition buck, try Greek yogurt.

Dark green, leafy vegetables, such as spinach, collards, kale, and chard, are packed with iron, calcium, and potassium, and vitamins A, C, E, and K.

Omega-3 fatty acids from fish, nuts, and seeds are healthy fats that help keep you fuller longer.

Plant-based milk is a wonderful alternative to dairy if you are trying to cut down on carbohydrates at a meal. They are easy to make but are also widely available at many stores. If you can, look for unsweetened versions.

Sweet potatoes, yams, and colored potatoes are high in antioxidants, vitamins, and fiber. They are more nutritious than white potatoes.

Whole grains are rich in magnesium, B vitamins, chromium, iron, folate, and fiber. Some of the heavy hitters in this category include farro, millet, quinoa, barley, and oats.

Foods to Eat in Moderation

These are the foods you need to approach with caution and eat less frequently, but remember, you don't have to avoid them entirely. An excess of the following foods and ingredients contributes to weight gain, increased blood sugar, and increase in the risk of heart disease. Although these foods get a bad rap, they are still food, and food is fuel. The reason these foods should be consumed less often is that they offer little nutritional value, are high in calories, may spike your blood sugar, or pose a health risk when eaten in abundance.

Eat less:

Saturated fats. Animal proteins, palm oil, coconut, and junk foods like chips, fried foods, and sweets contain these less-healthy fats.

Trans fats. Junk foods as well as packaged foods, margarine, frozen meals, muffins, and other baked goods contain trans fats because they lengthen the shelf life of food. Trans fats are linked to insulin resistance, heart disease, inflammation, and weight gain.

Cholesterol. High-cholesterol foods impact your heart. Keep red meats (such as beef, lamb, and pork) and some seafood (such as shrimp) to a minimum and consume lean meats. Eggs are an excellent source of protein, but the yolks contain nearly half your daily quota of cholesterol.

Sodium. High-sodium foods like deli meats, pickles, sauces, and condiments can increase your blood pressure and risk of hypertension.

Sugar-sweetened cereals. These increase your chances of high blood sugars.

Refined foods. White bread and white pasta are stripped of their original fiber, so they process much faster in the body and can spike our blood sugars.

When to Eat and How Often

Timing is everything, especially if you are taking medications to help manage your blood sugar. Eating around the same time, with four to six hours between larger meals, is highly recommended because your body can regulate your blood sugars more efficiently. Data suggest that making changes to promote more regular intake of energy during the day has positive effects on risk factors for heart disease and diabetes.

Breakfast should be the first meal of the day and never skipped. Eating within one to two hours of waking up will provide your body with the energy it needs to work more efficiently. When breakfast intake decreases, obesity and chronic disease increase. Several studies have proven this association, which is why eating breakfast is recommended as a strategy to reach a healthy body weight. Additionally, studies report negative side effects for those who skip breakfast. Their blood sugars remained high even after other meals in the day, they felt hungrier, and they typically ate more at the end of the day.

Although it can be tempting to snack late at night before bedtime, many studies would suggest you rethink eating that cookie. Late-night eating increased the risk of obesity and, combined with skipping breakfast, showed an increase in metabolic syndrome in a study of 60,800 people, ages 20 through 75. Metabolic syndrome is characterized by high blood pressure, high blood sugar, excess fat around the midline, and abnormal cholesterol levels.

Portioning Plates

Perhaps you've heard of MyPlate, the USDA's initiative that defines a healthy plate. It's an excellent place to start when thinking of how you could create balanced meals without having to crunch numbers and measure all your food. You're going to love how simple this tool is, because many Americans already eat in this fashion.

First of all, think of a 9-inch plate, not a 12-inch plate. Then divide your plate in half. This is your recommended nonstarchy vegetable portion, like leafy greens, tomatoes, eggplant, carrots, beets, onions,

Brussels sprouts, cauliflower, peppers, or cucumber. What remains are two quarters of the plate. One quarter is designated as the protein portion, including meats, cheese, tofu, or fish. Think about a deck of cards; this is a proper serving of protein at each meal. The remaining quarter is for starchy, carbohydrate foods such as whole grains and starchy vegetables like beans, peas, tubers, and potatoes. Lastly, beyond the well-organized plate, you can have a side serving of fruit, milk, or plant-based milk. It's truly that easy.

Not every meal you choose to eat will follow this system, but at least it's a good place to start so you don't feel overwhelmed. Eating can be challenging, so do what's most comfortable for you. If this simple system helps, then, by all means, use it.

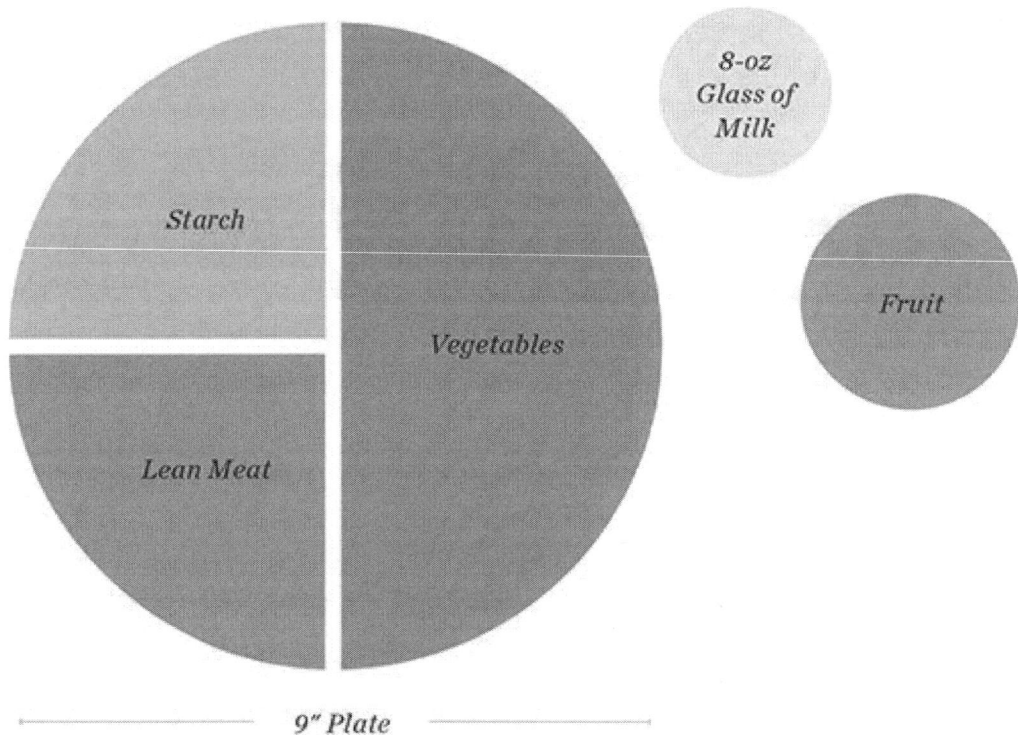

Setting Up Your Kitchen

Now let's take a moment to think about your kitchen so you can set yourself up for success. If you don't have the tools or space to create healthy meals, meal prep becomes challenging, so consider your kitchen setup. Is it a clean, welcoming space with room to prepare your foods? Clear your kitchen of mail, keys, clothes, and anything else that doesn't belong. Organization ensures your time in the kitchen is productive, safe, and fun! Countertops and surfaces used for cooking should be kept clean at all times. The easiest way to keep your kitchen fresh and tidy is to clean as you go. Wipe up spills as they occur and while you are cooking. There's typically a pause in most recipes, so use that time to put ingredients away in the pantry or wash dirty dishes.

Another critical element when setting up your kitchen is to make sure it is well stocked with food and equipment. This doesn't mean packing the space with products, it means having some essentials on hand and planning out your week of meals ahead of time when you can. If you run low on an ingredient or need a piece of equipment, write it down to remind yourself to purchase it the next time you go to the store. Before you start cooking, be sure to read through recipes in their entirety. It would be a bummer to have to run all the way back to the store after you've started cooking.

Foods to Stock

The most important part of your kitchen is the foods you stock. This means having a variety of ingredients that inspire you to cook and that you enjoy eating. These choices should store well in the freezer or pantry and allow you to make fast-and-easy meals. The bulk of these items should have a relatively long shelf life as well. Here's what I recommend.

REFRIGERATOR

- Cheese
- Citrus, such as lime, lemon, or orange

- Eggs
- Favorite sauces and condiments
- Fresh herbs
- Milk or plant-based milk
- Plain yogurt
- Variety of fresh produce

FREEZER

- Frozen vegetables
- Homemade broth and sauces
- Leftovers
- Protein (raw or cooked), including previously cooked beans and grains

PANTRY

Spices

- Black pepper
- Cayenne pepper
- Chili powder
- Cinnamon
- Cloves
- Cumin
- Dried herbs, such as rosemary, oregano, thyme, and bay leaves

- Fennel seeds

- Ground coriander

- Kosher salt

- Paprika

- Red pepper flakes

- Spice blends, such as Italian seasoning mix, taco seasoning, and curry powder

- Turmeric

Vegetables

- Garlic

- Onions

- Sweet potatoes

Oils and Vinegars

- Cider vinegar

- Extra-virgin olive oil

- Grapeseed or canola oil

- Red wine vinegar

Preserved Ingredients—low or no sodium added

- Canned cooked beans and lentils

- Canned tomatoes

- Canned tomato paste

- Canned tuna, fish, and chicken
- Canned vegetables

Starches

- Couscous
- Noodles, such as rice noodles, buckwheat, and macaroni
- Variety of dried beans and lentils
- Variety of whole grains, such as rice, bulgur, quinoa, and oats

Sauces and Condiments

- Broth
- Dijon mustard
- Honey
- Pasta sauce
- Salad dressings
- Salsa
- Tamari or soy sauce
- Unsweetened, unsalted peanut butter (or other nut butter)

Nuts and Seeds

- Almonds
- Chia seeds
- Flaxseed

- Peanuts

- Seeds, such as pumpkin, sesame, and sunflower

- Walnuts

Other Essentials

- Baking powder

- Baking soda

- Bouillon cubes, low-sodium

- Cocoa powder, unsweetened

- Coconut, shredded and unsweetened

- Dried fruits

- Lemon juice

- Powdered milk

- Tofu (refrigerated or shelf-stable)

Essential Equipment

Having gadgets and tools makes life more comfortable in the kitchen, but there is a point at which you can have too many. It can get expensive, and if you have limited storage space, that's also an issue. Here is a list of suggested equipment for your prediabetic kitchen, and keep in mind that if it's electronic, you can always do it the old fashioned way: by hand.

KITCHEN ESSENTIALS

- Baking sheets: two or three, and ideally identical, so they are easy to stack and store

- Blender

- Box grater: Can be used for zesting and shredding cheese and vegetables.

- Casserole dish or Dutch oven: Heatproof cookware is great to have, especially if it has a lid.

- Colander: Make sure the holes aren't too small if you want to double it up for rinsing grains, pasta, berries, or produce. Otherwise, get one with larger holes and another one with smaller holes.

- Cutting board: One large and one small will do the trick.

- Flat spatula: Use with nonstick pans.

- Kitchen shears

- Measuring cups and spoons: Accuracy is often crucial for recipe success, especially in baking.

- Mixing bowls: A combination of sizes that nest inside one another makes for better storage.

- Nonstick frying pan

- Pastry brush

- Saucepan: I recommend a 4-quart saucepan, the size commonly used for making sauces.

- Sharp knives: You don't need more than a chef's knife and a paring knife. Keep them sharp, too; a dull knife is more dangerous than a sharp one.

- Skillet: One medium to large in size, with a lid, will allow you to prepare many foods on the stove top.

- Stockpot: Get one with a fitted lid that's easy to lift.

- Thermometer: Use for meats to verify doneness.

- Vegetable peeler

- Whisk

- Wooden spoons

KITCHEN EXTRAS TO MAKE COOKING FASTER AND EASIER

- Bread knife: This blade is designed to cut bread but is also perfect for slicing through wraps, sandwiches, and tomatoes.

- Citrus juicer or reamer: This will make it easier to squeeze fresh citrus juice.

- Food processor: This appliance will save you boatloads of time on bean dips, doughs, and preparing vegetables.

- Immersion (hand-held) blender: This tool can be purchased with many attachments that allow you to whisk, process food in place of a food processor, and puree your foods. It's a great all-in-one electronic gadget.

- Mandoline: Allows you to get even, consistent slices every time.

- Microplane: This tool is for zesting citrus and grating hard cheeses, nutmeg, fresh ginger, and garlic cloves.

- Pressure cooker: Shortens the cooking time of whole grains, beans, stews, and meats.

- Salad spinner: Cleans your greens without using paper towels or cloth to dry them.

Where to Grocery Shop

Not sure where to shop for some of the pantry staples? Try your local co-ops, grocery stores, farmers' markets, and international markets.

The latter are generally family-run and not chains, which means you'll have to look them up online or ask around. You might be surprised by the ingredients found in these smaller stores. Typically, in larger US cities there is at least one market specializing in cuisines such as East Asian, Korean, African, Hispanic, or Indian. The food prices are generally lower, and you're supporting your local economy, so it's a win-win for the store and you. If you stick to larger grocery stores, visit the bulk-bin aisle to see what is available. Bulk items are often cheaper, and they allow you to experiment with new foods without committing to an entire bag of something you may not enjoy eating. Bring your own bags, containers, or glass jars to fill up in these sections. It's better for the environment, and it's nice to make sure sustainability is considered in your food purchases.

About the Recipes

Every recipe in this book will take 30 minutes or less from start to finish. In addition to time, much consideration was put toward variety, ease, plant-based foods, and availability of ingredients while emphasizing cross-culture recipes. It's how I eat and how I encourage others to eat. Some ingredients may seem exotic to you, like bison, but I'll guide you on alternatives while also challenging your taste buds to try something new. Don't let the names of foods or recipes fool you either. Don't ignore a recipe just because a title may include a word or food you are unfamiliar with; instead, use it as an opportunity to learn and expand your repertoire with new flavors. There are thousands of different foods available, and this book is meant to open your eyes to the possibilities.

Substitution recommendations are also offered, so you don't feel glued to a recipe. One of the most common things I hear about from patients is how stuck they feel when it comes to recipes. If one ingredient is missing, they throw their hands in the air and say, "Forget it, I can't do this!" I'm going to challenge you to look beyond the recipe, use my tips to make adjustments, and use the recipe as a guideline. Just like it takes time to make changes to your lifestyle, it is a process to become comfortable in the kitchen.

Lastly, feel free to adjust the salt and pepper in most of the recipes. You will decide if you want to omit the seasonings or add salt and pepper to taste. The idea behind this is to try the recipe as is and keep your sodium intake lower. But food should be enjoyable, and some recipes may need a pinch of salt or dash of black pepper to perk them up. I am confident you will love the recipes in this book—just as my patients have for years.

How They're Easy

The recipes in this book are meant to be quick, with little prep, to avoid having to stand for long periods in the kitchen. Most people do not want to spend their free time preparing food. I understand that spending more than 30 minutes on one meal is not compatible with a busy schedule. Extensive kitchen time is also not always possible for people who suffer from physical limitations.

These recipes are fast, easy, and use minimal kitchen equipment. You don't need a bunch of gadgets to make quick, healthy meals. Ingredients in this book should be easy to find at your local grocer. The recipes in this book also promote variety in your diet, so you can experience different flavors and ingredients with minimal effort and fuss.

Carb Counts and Nutritional Information

Looking at the nutritional information provided for the recipes is helpful if you know how to interpret it. Always take into account your portion size and multiply or divide if you do not eat the recommended serving. For example, if you consume an entire smoothie in a recipe and it is two servings, you need to multiply the data by two. The nutrition information you see listed is what you would find on an FDA nutrition label, which explains where the calories are coming from (carbohydrate, protein, and fat), then a further breaks down the common nutrients, vitamins, and minerals that are of concern in a standard American diet. As a prediabetic or diabetic, the primary macronutrient of concern is total carbohydrates. Work with a dietitian or CDCES to determine how many servings or total carbohydrates are appropriate for you.

In most cases, adults should not exceed 75 grams of carbohydrates per meal. It is more commonly recommended to have between three to five servings per meal, so 45 to 75 grams per meal. As we discussed, there are many types of carbohydrates, but all will affect your blood sugars. Fiber will have more of a stabilizing effect on your blood sugars, and any recipe containing more than 5 grams per serving is considered to be a "good source" of fiber.

Recipe Labels and Tips

All the recipes will be 30 minutes or less, with prep included. Amazing, right? Not only will you be guaranteed less time in the kitchen than your typical recipes, but there will be labels to help guide your decision to make it easy, too. Simply look for the following:

5-Ingredient: Recipes are made with five or fewer ingredients.

Gluten-Free: No gluten in the recipe; however, you'll want to read through the list of store-bought ingredients to make sure you have a gluten-free version. Tamari, Worcestershire sauce, miso, and certain grains like oats sometimes contain or come in contact with gluten.

High-Fiber: Contains 5 grams or more fiber per serving, which is great for keeping your blood sugars stabilized and keeping you fuller longer.

No-Cook: No heat necessary for these recipes. Simply chop, toss, and serve.

One Pot, One Pan, One Bowl: One and done, because it's nice to keep your cleanup to one thing.

Vegetarian: No meat, but can contain dairy, cheese, honey, or eggs. You'll find that many of these recipes are vegan, or easily made vegan, as well.

Look for these labels to help you see beyond the recipes and get creative, or to simply give you more information.

Ingredient Tip: How to best work with a particular ingredient.

Make It Easier: Shortcuts or kitchen tricks to make your cooking process even easier.

Nutrient Boost: My suggestions for adding extra nutrients to a recipe.

Substitution Tip: When and how you can substitute an ingredient for another.

Variation: Small recipe or ingredient changes for varying a recipe.

Easy Buckwheat Crêpes

CHAPTER THREE
Breakfast

Your morning meal becomes much easier and more enjoyable with these 16 reliable recipes. Most of the recipes in this chapter take less than 15 minutes to prepare, and you may be surprised to see that many include vegetables. Getting three to five servings of vegetables a day is challenging, but these recipes will help you integrate vegetables early in the day.

Breakfast foods are typically high in carbohydrates, and it can be hard to create a balance that keeps carbs in check. It's not that you *can't* eat them, but rather *how many* you consume in one meal. Think whole grains, and pair them with foods that do not spike your blood sugars, such as protein, nonstarchy vegetables, and fat, and you're on your way to a strong start to the day.

K

Blueberry-Chia Smoothie

Cherry, Chocolate, and Almond Shake

Stovetop Granola

Seedy Muesli

Overnight Oats

Apple Millet Porridge

Breakfast Banana Barley

Harvest Blackberry Quinoa Bowl

High-Protein Oatmeal

Carrot Cake Oatmeal

Strawberry-Ricotta Toast

Easy Buckwheat Crêpes

Shakshuka

Eggplant Breakfast Sandwich

Perfect Egg Scramble with Simple Salad

Avocado-Tofu Scramble with Roasted Potatoes

Blueberry-Chia Smoothie

Serves 2 / Prep time: 5 minutes

5-INGREDIENT, GLUTEN-FREE, HIGH-FIBER, NO-COOK, ONE POT,
VEGETARIAN

The blueberries in this delicious smoothie are a good source of vitamin C, an essential vitamin that also promotes wound healing. They are also high in fiber and manganese, which help the body better process cholesterol and carbohydrates. Couple that with chia seeds, a superfood high in omega fats and fiber, and you have a rich, fruity drink that is ideal for jump-starting your day.

2 cups frozen blueberries

½ medium frozen banana

2 tablespoons peanut butter

2 tablespoons chia seeds

12 ounces unsweetened soy milk, plus extra if needed

1. Combine the blueberries, banana, peanut butter, chia seeds, and soy mil blender and blend on high speed until smooth. Use a spatula to scrape d the sides as needed.

2. Serve immediately. If it's too thick, add more soy milk or water by the tablespoonful until you've reached the desired consistency.

VARIATION: Don't have blueberries on hand? Substitute any frozen berry, like strawberries or raspberries. Buy them in bulk when in season or on sale and freeze for later use. It will save you money in the long run, if you have the freezer space.

INGREDIENT TIP: I like to use ground chia seeds for this recipe for a smoother consistency. Simply grind them into a powder with a mini coffee grinder or mortar and pestle before using.

Per serving: Calories: 360; Total fat: 16g; Carbohydrates: 46g; Fiber: 14g; Protein: 12g; Calcium: 333mg; Vitamin D: 2mcg; Vitamin B$_{12}$: 2mcg; Iron: 2mg; Zinc: 1mg

Cherry, Chocolate, and Almond Shake

Serves 2 / Prep time: 5 minutes

5-INGREDIENT, GLUTEN-FREE, HIGH-FIBER, NO-COOK, ONE POT, VEGETARIAN

The combination of cherry, chocolate, and almond is perfect culinary harmony. Cherries have floral, spicy flavor notes, and their pits share a common flavor with almonds. This synchronicity makes the two ingredients sing together in unison. In fact, the molecule that is produced from both of these foods, called benzaldehyde, is the second most commonly used flavor molecule in the United States after vanillin. Adding the cocoa simply enhances a winning combination, balancing the sweetness with a hint of bitterness.

10 ounces frozen cherries

2 tablespoons cocoa powder

2 tablespoons almond butter

2 tablespoons hemp seeds

8 ounces unsweetened almond milk

Combine the cherries, cocoa, almond butter, hemp seeds, and almond milk in a blender and blend on high speed until smooth. Use a spatula to scrape down the sides as needed. Serve immediately.

VARIATION: You can also use cow's milk or another plant-based milk for this recipe; however, if you choose sweetened milk or use cow's milk, the carbohydrate content will increase.

Per serving: Calories: 284; Total fat: 16g; Carbohydrates: 32g; Fiber: 7g; Protein: 10g; Calcium: 308mg; Vitamin D: 1mcg; Vitamin B_{12}: 0mcg; Iron: 3mg; Zinc: 1mg

Stovetop Granola

Makes 4½ cups / Prep time: 10 minutes / Cook time: 10 minutes
ONE POT, VEGETARIAN

Most granola is baked in an oven, but that doesn't mean it can't be made on a stove top. Using a cast-iron skillet will create a toasted flavor that mimics the baked-in-the-oven taste. The recipe itself is written as a formula, so don't feel attached to specific ingredients. Keep it simple if you feel overwhelmed by building your own recipe; just use the first recommended ingredient in the list. Serve this granola with Greek yogurt for a complete breakfast, as a topping on a salad for extra crunch, or as a smoothie garnish.

1½ cups grains (rolled oats, rye flakes, or any flaked grain)

¼ cup vegetable, grapeseed, or extra-virgin olive oil

¼ cup honey or maple syrup

1 tablespoon spice (cinnamon, chai spices, turmeric, ginger, or cloves)

1 tablespoon citrus zest (orange, lemon, lime, or grapefruit) (optional)

1¼ cups roasted, chopped nuts (almonds, walnuts, or pistachios)

¾ cup seeds (sunflower, pumpkin, sesame, hemp, ground chia, or ground flaxseed)

½ cup dried fruit (golden raisins, apricots, raisins, dates, figs, or cranberries)

Kosher salt

1. Heat a large dry skillet, preferably cast iron, over medium-high heat. Ad grains and cook, stirring frequently, until golden brown and toasty. Rem the grains from the skillet and transfer them to a small bowl.

2. Reduce the heat to medium, return the skillet to the heat, and add the vegetable oil, honey, and spice. Stir until thoroughly combined and brin simmer.

3. Once the mixture begins to bubble, reduce the heat to low and add the c zest (if using), toasted grains, nuts, seeds, and dried fruit. Stir and cook f another 2 minutes or until the granola is sticky and you can smell the sp Adjust the seasonings as desired and add salt to taste.

4. Allow the granola to cool before storing it in an airtight container at roo temperature for up to 6 months.

VARIATION: Try these spice blends to encounter some new flavors. Combine in equal parts to get 1 tablespoon total for use in this recipe.

Savory: Red peppercorns, fennel seeds, bee pollen
Sweet: Cinnamon, cardamom, ginger
Green: Spirulina, matcha green tea powder
Earthy: Mushroom powder and beet powder

Per ¼-cup serving: Calories: 167; Total fat: 11g; Carbohydrates: 15g; Fiber: 3g; Protein: 4g; Calcium: 39mg; Vitamin D: 0mcg; Vitamin B$_{12}$: 0mcg; Iron: 1mg; Zinc: 1mg

Seedy Muesli

Makes 6 cups / Prep time: 5 minutes
GLUTEN-FREE, HIGH-FIBER, NO-COOK, ONE BOWL, VEGETARIAN

A popular breakfast in Sweden and Germany, muesli consists of raw rolled grains, dried fruit, nuts, and seeds. Muesli looks a lot like granola but does not contain sweeteners or oil, so it is kinder to your heart and blood sugars. Muesli is also easier to make—no baking or cooking required. When creating your own, choose from a variety of rolled grains but avoid quick-cooking varieties because those products are less nutritious. Allow the rolled grains to soften in yogurt or milk before consuming. You'll find more seeds and nuts in this than in a classic recipe; this version has fewer carbohydrates.

2 cups gluten-free rolled oats

1 cup roasted, slivered almonds

¾ cup raw sunflower seeds

½ cup raw pumpkin seeds

½ cup pistachios

½ cup apricots, sliced

¼ cup hemp seeds

¼ cup ground flaxseed

¼ cup toasted sesame seeds

1. In a medium bowl, combine the oats, almonds, sunflower seeds, pumpki seeds, pistachios, apricots, hemp seeds, flaxseed, and sesame seeds.

2. Store the mixture in an airtight container at room temperature for up to months.

SERVING SUGGESTION: In a bowl, combine ¾ cup of muesli with ½ cup of Greek yogurt and ¼ cup of milk or milk alternative (for lower carbohydrate total) and a few fresh strawberries.

VARIATION: Other rolled grains such as barley, rye, spelt, or rice can be substituted for rolled oats. Try adding different spices, like a tablespoon of nutmeg, cinnamon, or both, for exciting variations!

Per ¾-cup serving: Calories: 430; Total fat: 29g; Carbohydrates: 30g; Fiber: 8g; Protein: 16g; Calcium: 90mg; Vitamin D: 0mcg; Vitamin B$_{12}$: 0mcg; Iron: 4mg; Zinc: 2mg

Overnight Oats

Serves 1 / Prep time: 5 minutes
GLUTEN-FREE, NO-COOK, ONE BOWL, VEGETARIAN

Overnight oats are one of the easiest breakfasts to make: just mix and refrigerate, and then grab the finished creation as you run out the door. Not only is this breakfast effortless to make, but it also includes oats, which are a superfood because of their lower glycemic response compared with most other breakfast cereals. Oats are rich in beta-glucan, a type of fiber that reduces post-meal blood sugars and insulin responses, while delaying the absorption of carbs. This fiber also improves your gut's microbiome as a prebiotic. It's great for controlling blood sugars!

Base Recipe

¼ **cup rolled oats, gluten-free**

¼ **cup plain Greek yogurt**

¼ **cup plant-based milk**

Combine the oats, Greek yogurt, and plant-based milk in a single-serving jar at least 8 ounces in size. Mix well and store overnight or for at least 6 hours. Serve with the toppings of your choice.

Tahini, Maple, and Banana

¼ **cup plain Greek yogurt**

1 **tablespoon tahini**

1 **teaspoon maple syrup**

½ **banana, cut into rounds**

In a small bowl, combine the Greek yogurt, tahini, and maple syrup. Mix with the base recipe for overnight oats, put the mixture into a jar, and top it with banana. Place it in the refrigerator for at least 6 hours or overnight.

Tropical Mango

½ cup diced mango

2 tablespoons unsweetened coconut flakes

Top the base overnight oats recipe with mango and coconut before storing it in the refrigerator for at least 6 hours or overnight.

Make It Easier: This dish will keep for 4 days, so double or triple the recipe and you've got yourself breakfast all week.

Base recipe per serving: Calories: 138; Total fat: 4g; Carbohydrates: 17g; Fiber: 2g; Protein: 8g; Calcium: 188mg; Vitamin D: 1mcg; Vitamin B_{12}: <1mcg; Iron: 1mg; Zinc: 1mg

Tahini, Maple, and Banana per serving: Calories: 348; Total fat: 15g; Carbohydrates: 40g; Fiber: 5g; Protein: 17g; Calcium: 330mg; Vitamin D: 1mcg; Vitamin B_{12}: <1mcg; Iron: 3mg; Zinc: 2mg

Tropical Mango per serving: Calories: 253; Total fat: 11g; Carbohydrates: 31g; Fiber: 5g; Protein: 10g; Calcium: 200mg; Vitamin D: 1mcg; Vitamin B_{12}: <1mcg; Iron: 2mg; Zinc: 1mg

Apple Millet Porridge

Serves 2 / Prep time: 3 minutes / Cook time: 12 minutes
GLUTEN-FREE, HIGH-FIBER, ONE POT, VEGETARIAN

Millet is an unsung hero of the grain world—it's versatile, healthy, and delicious and yet often remains unknown. Here, millet is tastily paired with fresh apples and just a touch of honey to offer a healthy option for a warm morning meal. You will feel full and satiated all through the morning. If you have a bit more time on your hands, toast the millet by warming it up in a dry pan before starting the recipe. The natural nutty flavor will be enhanced, and it is well worth your time.

1 cup millet, rinsed and drained

2½ cups plant-based milk, divided

2 teaspoons ground cinnamon

Pinch kosher salt

1 tablespoon honey

1 apple, cored and cut into bite-size pieces

¼ cup chopped walnuts, toasted

1. In a small saucepan, combine the millet, 2 cups of milk, the cinnamon, a salt and place over medium heat. Cook, stirring until the millet puffs up fully cooked, 10 to 12 minutes.

2. Remove the millet from the heat and slowly add the remaining ½ cup o along with the honey. Adjust the seasonings as desired.

3. Divide the millet between two bowls and top each with half of the apple walnuts.

4. Store any leftovers in an airtight container in the refrigerator for up to 5

SUBSTITUTION TIP: You can substitute cow's milk in place of the plant-based milk for a creamier, richer porridge, or use water to cut back on calories and carbohydrates.

Per serving: Calories: 605; Total fat: 17g; Carbohydrates: 102g; Fiber: 14g; Protein: 15g; Calcium: 607mg; Vitamin D: 3mcg; Vitamin B_{12}: 0mcg; Iron: 5mg; Zinc: 2mg

Breakfast Banana Barley

Serves 2 / Prep time: 5 minutes / Cook time: 10 minutes
5-INGREDIENT, HIGH-FIBER, ONE POT, VEGETARIAN

Barley is another one of the world's grains that taste great and help keep you fuller longer. Its distinct flavor enhances the sweet banana and rich peanut butter in this recipe. Barley is loaded with fiber and is typically used in soups and stews, but who said it couldn't be eaten for breakfast? It is, after all, the world's oldest cultivated cereal, grown around the globe and used as a staple in many cuisines. This dish is especially filling, so save some for a snack later if you don't finish it all in one sitting.

3 cups water

Pinch kosher salt

1½ cups quick barley, rinsed and drained

3 tablespoons natural peanut butter

1 banana, sliced

1. In a small saucepan, bring the water and salt to a boil over high heat.

2. Stir in the barley, cover, reduce the heat, and simmer for 10 minutes or ι tender.

3. Remove the saucepan from the heat and add the peanut butter, stirring blend. Adjust the salt as desired, and divide the mixture between two bo

4. Top with the sliced bananas and serve.

5. Store any leftovers in an airtight container in the refrigerator for up to 5

VARIATION: Spice up this meal by adding some cinnamon, Chinese five-spice powder, or cardamom. This addition will really jazz up the flavor profile. Or, make it savory by omitting the banana and stirring in spinach or roasted vegetables.

Per serving: Calories: 725; Total fat: 14g; Carbohydrates: 136g; Fiber: 26g; Protein: 21g; Calcium: 58mg; Vitamin D: 0mcg; Vitamin B_{12}: 0mcg; Iron: 4mg; Zinc: 4mg

Harvest Blackberry Quinoa Bowl

Serves 2 / Prep time: 5 minutes / Cook time: 20 minutes
5-INGREDIENT, GLUTEN-FREE, HIGH-FIBER, ONE POT, VEGETARIAN

"Bowls" are all the rage at the moment. Not only do they offer an opportunity to mix a myriad of healthy and delicious ingredients together into one satiating product, but they also allow for some creativity in the kitchen. Quinoa and blackberry, with just a touch of cinnamon, is the breakfast bowl you never knew you needed. This bowl will keep in the refrigerator for five days and can be eaten cold or hot. To reheat, simply add some liquid and zap it in the microwave for 20- to 30-second intervals until heated through, or return it to the stove top. After it's cooked, add your berries and other desired toppings.

1½ cups water

Pinch kosher salt

¾ cup quinoa, rinsed

1 cup halved blackberries

Ground cinnamon, for garnish

1. In a medium saucepan, bring the water and salt to a boil over high heat, reduce the heat to low, and add the quinoa.

2. Cook until you see the grains are tender and the liquid is absorbed, abou minutes.

3. Remove the quinoa from the heat. If you prefer your quinoa to be fluffy, cover with a lid for a few minutes and allow it to rest. Once the quinoa is rested, use a fork to fluff it up, top it with the blackberries and a sprinkle cinnamon, and serve.

4. If you like your grains creamier, serve immediately topped with blackbe and cinnamon.

NUTRIENT BOOST: If you want extra protein in the morning, consider replacing the water in the recipe with plant-based milk. Otherwise, for extra protein replace the water with cow's milk.

Per serving: Calories: 286; Total fat: 3g; Carbohydrates: 53g; Fiber: 10g; Protein: 10g; Calcium: 51mg; Vitamin D: 0mcg; Vitamin B$_{12}$: 0mcg; Iron: 3mg; Zinc: <1mg

High-Protein Oatmeal

Serves 1 / Prep time: 2 minutes / Cook time: 8 minutes
5-INGREDIENT, GLUTEN-FREE, HIGH-FIBER, ONE POT, VEGETARIAN

This recipe was a part of my master's thesis in nutrition and it was the consistent favorite of all the many breakfast choices. The dish is high in protein, which is great for before or after a workout. You will find it simple and quick to prepare, and even though it is served warm, this fruit-and-nut-studded oatmeal is a great choice for any season.

8 ounces vanilla soy milk

½ cup oats

1 tablespoon chia seeds

¼ cup blueberries

1 tablespoon sliced and toasted almonds

1. In a medium saucepan over medium-high heat, stir together the soy mil oats.

2. Bring to a boil, reduce the heat to low, and simmer, stirring frequently, ι cooked and tender, 5 to 8 minutes.

3. Remove the oatmeal from the heat and serve topped with chia seeds, blueberries, and almonds.

4. Store any leftovers in an airtight container in the refrigerator for up to 5

VARIATION: Instead of vanilla soy milk, use any kind of milk and a small drop of vanilla extract to get the same flavor. Another easy swap is using frozen blueberries instead of fresh. Heat the frozen berries in a separate saucepan to thaw them and serve them hot, over the oats, garnished with chia seeds and almonds.

Per serving: Calories: 373; Total fat: 13g; Carbohydrates: 49g; Fiber: 12g; Protein: 15g; Calcium: 420mg; Vitamin D: 3mcg; Vitamin B_{12}: 3mcg; Iron: 3mg; Zinc: 2mg

Carrot Cake Oatmeal

Serves 1 / Prep time: 3 minutes / Cook time: 10 minutes
GLUTEN-FREE, HIGH-FIBER, ONE POT, VEGETARIAN

Carrot cake is one of my mother's all-time favorite desserts. However, she's allergic to eggs, so I had to come up with something special to fulfill her craving. Better yet, this dish is something she can enjoy at breakfast reminiscent of her favorite dessert. The creaminess of the almond butter with hints of sweetness from the raisins and shredded carrot will certainly remind you of the classic cake, but rest assured, this is the ideal nutritious breakfast treat.

½ cup unsweetened almond milk

½ cup water

1 carrot, grated

⅓ cup rolled oats

1 tablespoon golden raisins

1 teaspoon honey

Pinch ground cinnamon

1½ tablespoons almond butter

½ cup cottage cheese

1. In a small saucepan, combine the almond milk, water, grated carrot, oat golden raisins, honey, and cinnamon over medium heat. Bring the mixtu a boil, reduce the heat to low, and simmer, stirring occasionally, until th are cooked, about 7 minutes.

2. Mix in the almond butter, remove the saucepan from the heat, and trans the oats to a bowl.

3. Serve immediately, topped with cottage cheese.

4. Store any leftovers in an airtight container in the refrigerator for up to 5

SUBSTITUTION TIP: To make this tempting breakfast vegan, substitute agave nectar for the honey and skip the cottage cheese altogether.

Per serving: Calories: 445; Total fat: 21g; Carbohydrates: 47g; Fiber: 7g; Protein: 21g; Calcium: 431mg; Vitamin D: 1mcg; Vitamin B$_{12}$: <1mcg; Iron: 3mg; Zinc: 2mg

Strawberry-Ricotta Toast

Serves 1 / Prep time: 5 minutes

5-INGREDIENT, HIGH-FIBER, NO-COOK, ONE BOWL, VEGETARIAN

This dish looks decadent with sweet strawberries and rich, cloud-like ricotta cheese, but is as light and nutritious as anything else in the book. Recipes like this one illustrate just how delectable natural foods can be, and how added sugar isn't necessary for a meal that will satisfy your sweet tooth. When strawberries are out of season, choose pears or other seasonal fruit as a substitute. The ricotta cheese on the toast acts like a glue for the fruit, so make sure to dice up whichever fruit you use into small, bite-size pieces.

2 slices whole-grain bread, toasted

½ cup ricotta cheese

2 cups diced strawberries

3 tablespoons toasted chopped hazelnuts

2 tablespoons chopped fresh mint (optional)

1. Place the toast on your work surface and evenly divide the ricotta betwe the slices, spreading it out to cover the bread.

2. Top each slice with the strawberries, hazelnuts, and mint (if using), ever distributing the ingredients on the cheese.

3. Serve immediately.

VARIATION: No hazelnuts on hand? Try other nuts and seeds like almonds, walnuts, poppy seeds, hemp seeds, or pumpkin seeds. Otherwise, serve it with a salad from this book.

Per serving: Calories: 634; Total fat: 30g; Carbohydrates: 73g; Fiber: 13g; Protein: 25g; Calcium: 465mg; Vitamin D: <1mcg; Vitamin B_{12}: 1mcg; Iron: 5mg; Zinc: 3mg

Easy Buckwheat Crêpes

Makes 12 crêpes / Prep time: 5 minutes / Cook time: 15 minutes
5-INGREDIENT, GLUTEN-FREE, ONE PAN, VEGETARIAN

Traditional crêpes are very thin, cooked pancakes that originated from the northwest region of Brittany, France. As these tasty pancakes gained popularity, the recipe was revamped using wheat flour instead of buckwheat because this grain was more prevalent in many regions. When they're made into a savory version, called a galette, buckwheat flour is traditionally used. Many sweeter versions of crêpes are made with all-purpose flour, eggs, milk, and butter. What I love most about this recipe is its versatility. You can create sweet or savory crêpes with different fillings, including scrambled eggs, deli meats, cured fish, fresh fruit, cheese, nut butter, or roasted vegetables. The choice is yours!

1 cup buckwheat flour

1¾ cups milk

⅛ teaspoon kosher salt

1 tablespoon extra-virgin olive oil

½ tablespoon ground flaxseed (optional)

1. Combine the buckwheat flour, milk, salt, extra-virgin olive oil, and flaxs[...] using), in a bowl and whisk thoroughly, or in a blender and pulse until w[...] combined.

2. Heat a nonstick medium skillet over medium heat. Once it's hot, add a ¼[...] of batter to the skillet, spreading it out evenly. Cook until bubbles appea[...] the edges crisp like a pancake, 1 to 3 minutes, then flip and cook for anot[...] minutes.

3. Repeat until all the batter is used up, and the crêpes are cooked. Layer parchment paper or tea towels between the crêpes to keep them from sticking to one another while also keeping them warm until you're read[...] eat.

4. Serve with the desired fillings.

5. Store any leftovers in an airtight container in the refrigerator for up to ₹

MAKE IT EASIER: If the batter starts sticking to the skillet, use a little cooking oil or spray before making each crêpe.

Per 2-crêpe serving: Calories: 130; Total fat: 5g; Carbohydrates: 18g; Fiber: 2g; Protein: 5g; Calcium: 89mg; Vitamin D: 1mcg; Vitamin B_{12}: <1mcg; Iron: 1mg; Zinc: 1mg

Shakshuka

Serves 4 / Prep time: 5 minutes / Cook time: 25 minutes
HIGH-FIBER, VEGETARIAN

This is one of my absolute favorite breakfasts. It is savory and satisfying and creates an incredible choir of flavors when the garlic, harissa, and coriander harmonize with the tomato base. This recipe is influenced by the incredible food culture of Israel. It manages to be just as flavorful as anything with bacon or sausage on the side, and it's much lighter. Some versions are green, which comes from the addition of zucchini, spinach, or tomatillos (in place of the tomatoes). Throw in a handful of spinach to this recipe to boost your iron.

2 tablespoons extra-virgin olive oil

1 onion, diced

2 tablespoons tomato paste

2 red bell peppers, diced

2 tablespoons Harissa (optional)

4 garlic cloves, minced

2 teaspoons ground cumin

½ teaspoon ground coriander (optional)

1 teaspoon smoked paprika

2 (14-ounce) cans diced tomatoes

4 large eggs

½ cup plain Greek yogurt

Bread, for dipping (optional)

1. Heat the extra-virgin olive oil in a Dutch oven or large saucepan over me heat. When it starts to shimmer, add the onion and cook until transluce about 3 minutes.

2. Add the tomato paste, peppers, harissa (if using), garlic, cumin, coriand using), paprika, and tomatoes. Bring to a simmer and cook 10 to 15 min

until the peppers are cooked and the sauce is thick. Adjust the seasonin; desired.

3. Make four wells in the mixture with the back of a large spoon and gentl; break one egg into each well. Cover the saucepan and simmer gently un egg whites are set but the yolks are still runny, 5 to 8 minutes.

4. Remove the saucepan from the heat and spoon the tomato mixture and cooked egg into each of four bowls. Top with the Greek yogurt and serve bread (if using).

SUBSTITUTION TIP: If you want to keep it classic and you have access to a Middle Eastern grocery store, look for labneh in place of Greek yogurt. It's creamy, slightly sour, and cheese-like. Also, consider turning up the heat and adding the optional harissa, or cayenne or red pepper flakes.

Per serving: Calories: 259; Total fat: 14g; Carbohydrates: 22g; Fiber: 6g; Protein: 12g; Calcium: 88mg; Vitamin D: 1mcg; Vitamin B_{12}: 1mcg; Iron: 2mg; Zinc: 1mg

Eggplant Breakfast Sandwich

Serves 2 to 4 / Prep time: 5 minutes / Cook time: 20 minutes
GLUTEN-FREE, HIGH-FIBER, VEGETARIAN

Eggplant isn't a common breakfast ingredient, but this vegetable works well here as an alternative for bread. Crispy on the outside, creamy in the center, with runny egg oozing from the sides, this is a breakfast sandwich you will crave. You may want two, so plan accordingly if you are hungry or want to indulge in a breakfast that won't break the calorie bank.

2 tablespoons extra-virgin olive oil, divided

1 eggplant, cut into 8 (½-inch-thick) rounds

¼ teaspoon kosher salt

¼ teaspoon freshly ground black pepper

4 large eggs

1 garlic clove, minced

4 cups fresh baby spinach

Hot sauce or Harissa (optional)

1. Heat 1 tablespoon of extra-virgin olive oil in a large skillet over medium Add the eggplant in a single layer and cook until tender and browned on sides, 4 to 5 minutes per side. Transfer the eggplant from the skillet to a and season it with salt and pepper. Wipe out the skillet and set aside.

2. Meanwhile, place a large saucepan filled three-quarters full with water (medium-high heat and bring it to a simmer. Carefully break the eggs int small, individual bowls and pour slowly into a fine-mesh strainer over another bowl. Allow the excess white to drain, then lower the strainer ir the water. Tilt the egg out into the water. Repeat with the remaining egg Swirl the water occasionally as the eggs cook and whites set, about 4 mir Remove the eggs with a slotted spoon, transfer them to a paper towel, ar drain.

3. Heat the remaining 1 tablespoon of extra-virgin olive oil over medium h the large skillet and add the garlic and spinach. Cook until the spinach i:

wilted, about 1 minute.

4. Place one eggplant round on each of four plates and evenly divide the sp
among the rounds. Top the spinach with a poached egg on each sandwic
place the remaining eggplant round on the egg. Serve with hot sauce or
harissa (if using).

Per serving: Calories: 362; Total fat: 25g; Carbohydrates: 21g; Fiber: 10g; Protein: 17g; Calcium: 138mg; Vitamin D: 2mcg; Vitamin B_{12}: 1mcg; Iron: 4mg; Zinc: 2mg

Perfect Egg Scramble with Simple Salad

Serves 4 / Prep time: 17 minutes / Cook time: 5 minutes
GLUTEN-FREE, VEGETARIAN

This is my version of a light and fluffy egg scramble. Waiting the 15 minutes for the eggs to sit with the salt is well worth it. This method not only prevents your eggs from becoming runny on your plate, but it also enhances the taste. These eggs pair beautifully with a simple salad made with any greens you have on hand. If you don't like the spiciness of arugula, try this with leaf lettuce or mixed baby greens.

8 large eggs

3 tablespoons milk

Kosher salt

6 cups arugula

1 tablespoon extra-virgin olive oil

2 tablespoons minced red onion

1 bunch radishes, thinly sliced

1 lemon, cut into wedges

2 tablespoons unsalted butter

1. In a medium bowl, whisk the eggs, milk, and a pinch of salt until blended aside for 15 minutes.

2. Meanwhile, in a large bowl, toss the arugula with the extra-virgin olive onion, radishes, and a pinch of salt. Evenly divide the salad among four and garnish each with a lemon wedge.

3. Melt the butter in a medium nonstick skillet over medium-high heat. Ac eggs to the skillet and cook by scraping the bottom very slowly, then fol Repeat until the eggs have formed solid, moist curds. Portion the scram eggs evenly among the plates and serve immediately.

MAKE IT EASIER: Try using a mandoline to easily slice the radishes very thinly. Always use the guard that comes with this kitchen tool to protect your fingers from the blades.

Per serving: Calories: 262; Total fat: 20g; Carbohydrates: 6g; Fiber: 2g; Protein: 14g; Calcium: 128mg; Vitamin D: 2mcg; Vitamin B$_{12}$: 1mcg; Iron: 2mg; Zinc: 1mg

Avocado-Tofu Scramble with Roasted Potatoes

Serves 4 / Prep time: 5 minutes / Cook time: 25 minutes
GLUTEN-FREE, VEGETARIAN

Crumbled tofu makes for a perfect scrambled egg replacement that's so easy to cook. The slightly curdled appearance and taste from the added spices mimic scrambled eggs quite effectively. The roasted potatoes side in this recipe is also ideal for some of the other breakfast recipes in this book. Look for colored varieties, which have more nutrients than white potatoes. Try turnips, rutabagas, or other root vegetables as healthier substitutes for potatoes as well.

1½ pounds small potatoes, cut into bite-size pieces

4 tablespoons plant-based oil (safflower, olive, or grapeseed), divided

Kosher salt

Freshly ground black pepper

1 ounce water

2 teaspoons ground cumin

2 teaspoons turmeric

¼ teaspoon paprika

1 yellow onion, finely chopped

1 bell pepper, finely chopped

3 cups kale, torn into bite-size pieces

3 ounces firm tofu, drained and crumbled

1 avocado, diced, for garnish

1. Preheat the oven to 425°F. Line a baking sheet with parchment paper.

2. Combine the potatoes with 2 tablespoons of oil and a pinch each of salt ِ pepper on the baking sheet, then toss them to coat. Roast for 20 to 25 m or until tender and golden brown.

3. Meanwhile, stir together the water, cumin, turmeric, and paprika until ِ mixed to make the sauce. Set aside.

4. Heat the remaining 2 tablespoons of oil in a large skillet over medium h Add the onion and bell pepper and sauté for 3 to 5 minutes. Season with pinch of salt and pepper.

5. Add the kale to the skillet, cover, and allow the steam to cook the kale fo about 2 minutes.

6. Remove the lid and, using a spatula, push the vegetables to one side of th skillet and place the tofu and sauce on the empty side. Stir until the tofu heated through, 3 to 5 minutes. Stir the tofu and vegetables.

7. Serve the tofu scramble with the roasted potatoes on the side and garni with avocado.

MAKE IT EASIER: If you have time, allowing the tofu to dry out as much as possible will make it easier to crumble it. Placing the tofu between clean kitchen towels can speed up this process considerably.

Per serving: Calories: 256; Total fat: 10g; Carbohydrates: 36g; Fiber: 7g; Protein: 7g; Calcium: 114mg; Vitamin D: 0mcg; Vitamin B$_{12}$: 0mcg; Iron: 4mg; Zinc: 1mg

Grilled Romaine with White Beans

CHAPTER FOUR
Salad

Salads are often considered an afterthought, but they can be a meal in and of themselves. They're also great as a quick side, especially when trying to sneak some veggies into your meal. Salad ends up on my plate for almost every meal to help ensure I reach my recommended three to five servings per day. If the following recipes have two serving-size recommendations, the larger number applies to the dish as a side and the smaller number applies to the dish as a main. Get creative and mix and match the dressings by paging forward to the Seasonings, Sauces, and Dressings chapter. You can also keep it simple—if you don't have a dressing handy, simply squeeze on fresh citrus juice and a drizzle of extra-virgin olive oil.

a

Citrus Avocado Salad

Herbed Tomato Salad

Spinach Salad with Strawberries and Toasted Almonds

Asparagus Salad with Chile-Lime Dressing

Kale Caesar Salad

Pomegranate "Tabbouleh" with Cauliflower

Shaved Brussels Sprouts and Kale with Poppy Seed Dressing

Quinoa and Cucumber Salad

Apple-Bulgur Salad

Sweet Beet Grain Bowl

Grilled Romaine with White Beans

Chickpea Fattoush Salad

Roasted Carrot and Quinoa with Goat Cheese

Citrus Avocado Salad

Serves 2 / Prep time: 10 minutes

GLUTEN-FREE, HIGH FIBER, NO-COOK, ONE BOWL, VEGETARIAN

Looking for something bright and sunny that will leave you feeling fresh and rejuvenated? This recipe is ideal for a brunch side or for adding extra vitamin C to your day. The granola offers much-needed crunch, but it is 100 percent optional. You can substitute something else to provide the desired crispy texture like toasted pistachios, almonds, or sunflower seeds. Need more options? Serve the salad with whole-grain crackers or cooked grains.

4 cups salad greens

1 grapefruit, peeled and segmented

1 orange, peeled and segmented

2 tablespoons minced red onion

¼ cup fresh mint leaves, torn

3 tablespoons Lemon Vinaigrette Dressing or store-bought

1 avocado, thinly sliced

¼ cup Stovetop Granola (optional)

In a medium bowl, toss together the salad greens, grapefruit, orange, red onion, mint, and dressing. Arrange the salad on a plate with the slices of avocado and a sprinkling of granola (if using).

VARIATION: Try the Tahini Dressing or Poppy Seed Dressing as an alternative to the lemon vinaigrette, or make prep easier by drizzling extra-virgin olive oil on top if you don't have a dressing on hand or the time to make it.

Per serving: Calories: 364; Total fat: 26g; Carbohydrates: 32g; Fiber: 9g; Protein: 6g; Calcium: 148mg; Vitamin D: 0mcg; Vitamin B$_{12}$: 0mcg; Iron: 5mg; Zinc: 1mg

Herbed Tomato Salad

Serves 2 to 4 / Prep time: 7 minutes

GLUTEN-FREE, NO-COOK, ONE BOWL, VEGETARIAN

This bright and herbaceous salad is an excellent complement to the Perfect Egg Scramble or your favorite sandwich. I look forward to tomato season all year. Tomatoes are a vibrant ingredient available year-round in the grocery store, but they are at their best late summer and early fall. They contain vitamin C, antioxidants, fiber, potassium, and folate that may help prevent cancer and support heart health.

1 pint cherry tomatoes, halved

1 bunch fresh parsley, leaves only (stems discarded)

1 cup cilantro, leaves only (stems discarded)

¼ cup fresh dill

1 teaspoon sumac (optional)

2 tablespoons extra-virgin olive oil

Kosher salt

Freshly ground black pepper

1. In a medium bowl, carefully toss together the tomatoes, parsley, cilantr sumac (if using), extra-virgin olive oil, and salt and pepper to taste.

2. Store any leftovers in an airtight container in the refrigerator for up to : but the salad is best consumed on the day it is dressed.

SUBSTITUTION TIP: If you don't have all the herbs listed, you can substitute other herbs, such as tarragon or mint. Most herbs taste delicious in this recipe, so use what you have on hand.

INGREDIENT TIP: If you have a green thumb, grow heirloom varieties of cherry tomatoes to save money. They make wonderful snacks and can quench your thirst as you wander through the garden.

Per serving: Calories: 161; Total fat: 14g; Carbohydrates: 8g; Fiber: 3g; Protein: 3g; Calcium: 65mg; Vitamin D: 0mcg; Vitamin B$_{12}$: 0mcg; Iron: 3mg; Zinc: 1mg

Spinach Salad with Strawberries and Toasted Almonds

Serves 2 to 4 / Prep time: 7 minutes

5-INGREDIENT, GLUTEN-FREE, HIGH FIBER, NO-COOK, ONE BOWL, VEGETARIAN

Strawberry-spinach salad with balsamic or poppy seed dressing is a classic, so you have probably come across it at some point. It's a crowd-pleaser for sure, but the recipe can be improved. This is my version of the strawberry salad—with the addition of chopped toasted almonds, you get a boost of nutrition, flavor, and crunch.

8 cups packed fresh baby spinach

16 strawberries, quartered

4 ounces goat cheese, crumbled

¼ cup chopped toasted almonds

2 tablespoons Lemon Vinaigrette Dressing or store-bought

Kosher salt

Freshly ground black pepper

1. In a bowl, gently toss together the spinach, strawberries, goat cheese, ar almonds. Drizzle the salad with the vinaigrette and season with salt and pepper to taste.

2. Store any leftovers in an airtight container in the refrigerator for up to ? but the salad is best consumed on the day it is dressed.

VARIATION: Try different greens like arugula, mizuna, mixed greens, or romaine instead of spinach or create a blend of greens for a delicious complexity in flavor and texture.

Per serving: Calories: 516; Total fat: 39g; Carbohydrates: 21g; Fiber: 8g; Protein: 25g; Calcium: 694mg; Vitamin D: <1mcg; Vitamin B$_{12}$: <1mcg; Iron: 6mg; Zinc: 2mg

Asparagus Salad with Chile-Lime Dressing

Serves 2 to 4 / Prep time: 15 minutes
GLUTEN-FREE, HIGH-FIBER, NO-COOK, VEGETARIAN

Asparagus was proclaimed by Queen Nefertiti as the "food of the Gods," and when you taste this hearty salad, you will understand why. The elegant slender vegetable harkens the end of winter with its appearance at farmers' markets in the spring. For this recipe, you'll peel the stalks into ribbons, which you can do using a vegetable peeler. This salad highlights the addictive crunch of asparagus and the heat of the chile in the dressing. Studies suggest asparagus may also improve your body's ability to lower blood sugar naturally, so it's great to include in any meal.

1 bunch asparagus, woody ends trimmed and stalks peeled into ribbons

12 ounces leftover rotisserie chicken (optional)

2 cups shredded cabbage

1 cup arugula

1 bunch (about 8) radishes, thinly sliced

½ cup mint, stemmed and finely sliced

3 scallions, both white and green parts, finely sliced

¼ to ½ cup Chile-Lime Dressing or store-bought

⅓ cup chopped, roasted (unsalted) peanuts

Pickled Red Onions (optional)

1. Combine the asparagus ribbons, chicken (if using), cabbage, arugula, radishes, mint, and scallions in a large bowl. Pour the dressing in and to combine with your hands or tongs.

2. Place the salad on a large serving plate and garnish it with the chopped peanuts, pickled red onions, and more chopped mint if you like.

INGREDIENT TIP: Prepping asparagus can take a little extra time because you have to remove the lower fibrous portion of the stalk. The best method is to bend the stalk and let it snap at the natural spot, then line up the remaining stalks and cut them at the same place.

VARIATION: Try using different types of cabbage in this recipe: red, green, napa, or savoy! Each variety adds a unique taste, appearance, and texture to the dish.

Per serving: Calories: 391; Total fat: 30g; Carbohydrates: 25g; Fiber: 10g; Protein: 13g; Calcium: 147mg; Vitamin D: 0mcg; Vitamin B_{12}: 0mcg; Iron: 7mg; Zinc: 2mg

Kale Caesar Salad

Serves 2 to 4 / Prep time: 8 minutes / Cook time: 15 minutes
GLUTEN-FREE, HIGH-FIBER

Caesar salad is something of a staple in American restaurants. It has been prepared since Prohibition, when it was invented at Caesar's restaurant in Tijuana, Mexico. However, the traditional ingredients can be altered to create exciting new salads with the same spirit. This spin-off of the classic romaine version, featuring hearty kale instead, reminds us how versatile leafy greens can be in recipes.

FOR THE OAT CROUTONS

½ cup rolled oats

1 tablespoon sunflower seeds

1 tablespoon chopped almonds

1 tablespoon canola oil

1 tablespoon honey

Pinch kosher salt

FOR THE SALAD

1 bunch kale, cleaned, ribs removed, and chopped

1 bunch fresh parsley, leaves only

¼ cup Parmesan cheese

¼ to ½ cup Caesar Dressing or store-bought

1 lemon, cut into wedges (optional)

TO MAKE THE OAT CROUTONS

1. Preheat the oven to 350°F.

2. In a small bowl, combine the oats, sunflower seeds, almonds, oil, honey, pinch of salt. Toss to coat evenly, then spread the mixture on a nonstick baking sheet. Bake for 12 to 15 minutes, then remove from the oven to c(the baking sheet for 15 minutes.

TO MAKE THE SALAD

3. Meanwhile, in a large bowl, toss the kale, parsley, and Parmesan cheese the Caesar dressing until all the leaves are coated. Arrange the salad on and garnish with the lemon wedges (if using).

4. Top the salad with the croutons and serve.

5. If the dressing and oats are kept separately from the greens, then the sal and dressing will keep separately for 5 days in airtight containers in the refrigerator. The croutons will keep in an airtight container in the refrigerator for up to 1 month.

MAKE IT EASIER: The oat croutons are higher in protein and fiber compared to your standard crouton made from bread. If you want to forget the croutons and just eat the greens, no problem.

Per serving: Calories: 340; Total fat: 20g; Carbohydrates: 31g; Fiber: 6g; Protein: 12g; Calcium: 307mg; Vitamin D: <1mcg; Vitamin B_{12}: <1mcg; Iron: 4mg; Zinc: 2mg

Pomegranate "Tabbouleh" with Cauliflower

Serves 4 to 6 / Prep time: 20 minutes / Cook time: 5 minutes
GLUTEN-FREE, HIGH-FIBER, VEGETARIAN

Pomegranate seeds, or arils, add a slight sweetness to this fantastic take on tabbouleh salad. Traditional tabbouleh calls for bulgur. Here, I take a bit lighter and gluten-free approach by substituting finely chopped cauliflower for the more filling grain. If you are looking for a quick late-night meal, whip this up in less than 30 minutes and enjoy. Rest assured, if you aren't worried about gluten or would prefer to use bulgur, you can substitute it for the cauliflower or add it as an extra ingredient.

⅓ **cup extra-virgin olive oil, divided**

4 cups grated cauliflower (about 1 medium head)

Juice of 1 lemon

¼ **red onion, minced**

4 large tomatoes, diced

3 large bunches flat-leaf parsley, chopped

1 large bunch mint, chopped

½ **cup pomegranate arils**

Kosher salt

Freshly ground black pepper

1. In a large skillet, heat 2 tablespoons of extra-virgin olive oil. When it's h add the cauliflower and sauté for 3 to 5 minutes or until it starts to crisp Remove the skillet from the heat and allow the cauliflower to cool while prep the remaining ingredients.

2. In a large bowl, combine the remaining extra-virgin olive oil with the le juice and red onion. Mix well, then mix in the tomatoes, parsley, mint, a pomegranate arils.

3. After the cauliflower cools, 5 to 7 minutes, add it to the bowl with the otl ingredients. Season with salt and pepper to taste and serve.

4. Store any leftovers in an airtight container in the refrigerator for 3 to 5 (

SUBSTITUTION TIP: Pomegranates may be challenging to find. Omit them completely or substitute diced strawberries for a similar sweet taste and pop of red color.

Per serving: Calories: 270; Total fat: 19g; Carbohydrates: 22g; Fiber: 8g; Protein: 7g; Calcium: 146mg; Vitamin D: 0mcg; Vitamin B$_{12}$: 0mcg; Iron: 5mg; Zinc: 1mg

Shaved Brussels Sprouts and Kale with Poppy Seed Dressing

Serves 4 to 6 / Prep time: 20 minutes

5-INGREDIENT, GLUTEN-FREE, HIGH-FIBER, NO-COOK, ONE BOWL, VEGETARIAN

Brussels sprouts are making a comeback, but not as the notoriously overcooked army of small cabbages. They have earned their place alongside other classic greens in their raw form, as a hearty and tasty salad base. The fastest method of preparing Brussels sprouts is to use a mandoline. This kitchen utensil features two wickedly sharp parallel blades that you slide the vegetables over to produce shreds, slices, and even crinkle cuts. Be very slow and cautious with this tool, so you don't nick your finger. You can also use a knife to thinly slice the Brussels sprouts, halving them lengthwise before cutting into slices.

1 pound Brussels sprouts, shaved

1 bunch kale, thinly shredded

4 scallions, both white and green parts, thinly sliced

4 ounces shredded Romano cheese

<u>Poppy Seed Dressing</u> **or store-bought**

Kosher salt

Freshly ground black pepper

In a large bowl, toss together the Brussels sprouts, kale, scallions, and Romano cheese. Add the dressing to the greens and toss to combine. Season with salt and pepper to taste.

NUTRITION BOOST: Bulk up with protein in this salad by adding hard-boiled eggs, almonds, shredded chicken, or cooked chickpeas.

Per serving: Calories: 251; Total fat: 12g; Carbohydrates: 23g; Fiber: 6g; Protein: 14g; Calcium: 413mg; Vitamin D: <1mcg; Vitamin B$_{12}$: <1mcg; Iron: 2mg; Zinc: 1mg

Quinoa and Cucumber Salad

Serves 2 to 4 / Prep time: 10 minutes / Cook time: 15 minutes
GLUTEN-FREE, HIGH-FIBER, VEGETARIAN

Quinoa is another one of those superfoods or "super grains" that you should work to include in your diet. It's one of the few plant-based foods that contain all the essential amino acids, the building blocks of proteins that play critical roles in your body. Quinoa is loaded with protein and fiber, is gluten-free, and is a wonderful substitute for rice because it doesn't have as many carbohydrates by volume. It is also being studied for its role in diabetes and hypertension management because of its rich antioxidant level.

1 cup quinoa, rinsed

2 cups water

Kosher salt

Freshly ground black pepper

1 bunch fresh parsley, minced

1 medium cucumber, cut into ¼-inch dice

¼ cup minced red onion

2 tablespoons toasted sesame seeds

¼ to ½ cup Tahini Dressing or store-bought

4 ounces crumbled feta

1. In a small saucepan, combine the quinoa with the water and a pinch eac salt and pepper. Bring to a boil over medium-high heat, then decrease tc gentle simmer and allow to cook for 10 to 15 minutes, or until the quino; absorbed all the water. Remove the pot from the heat, cover, and allow t

2. Meanwhile, in a large bowl, mix together the parsley, cucumber, red oni sesame seeds, and dressing.

3. Once the quinoa is fully cooked, add it to the bowl with the other ingred Toss to coat evenly and season with salt and pepper.

4. Top the salad with feta and serve.

5. Store any leftovers in an airtight container in the refrigerator for 3 to 5 (

SUBSTITUTION TIP: Don't have quinoa? Use another grain instead. Any leftover grain will do in a pinch, such as wild rice, brown rice, quinoa, millet, bulgur, or buckwheat.

Per serving: Calories: 653; Total fat: 27g; Carbohydrates: 78g; Fiber: 13g; Protein: 25g; Calcium: 439mg; Vitamin D: <1mcg; Vitamin B_{12}: 1mcg; Iron: 8mg; Zinc: 4mg

Apple-Bulgur Salad

Serves 2 / Prep time: 10 minutes / Cook time: 15 minutes
HIGH-FIBER, VEGETARIAN

You might have noticed an abundance of grains in this salad section. Salads are more than just greens and dressing, and adding grains turn salads into full meals that fill you up and keep you that way. This recipe uses bulgur, which soaks up the zing of vinegar incredibly well, balancing the sweet flavor of apple. Apples taste best in the autumn, when they are in season. You can plan a special outing at a local orchard to buy boatloads of apples or pick your own. If apples aren't your favorite, there are plenty of other fruits that work beautifully in this recipe, such as persimmons, kumquats, pears, grapes, or oranges.

2 cups water

1 cup bulgur

1 teaspoon dried thyme

2 tablespoons extra-virgin olive oil

2 teaspoons cider vinegar

Kosher salt

Freshly ground black pepper

6 kale leaves, shredded

1 small apple, cored and diced

3 tablespoons sliced, toasted almonds

1. In a large saucepan, bring the water to a boil over high heat and remove from the heat. Add the bulgur and thyme, cover, and allow the grain to r 7 to 15 minutes or until cooked through.

2. Meanwhile, in a large bowl, whisk together the extra-virgin olive oil and vinegar with a pinch of salt and pepper. Add the cooked bulgur, kale, ap and almonds to the dressing and toss to combine. Adjust the seasonings desired.

3. Store any leftovers in an airtight container in the refrigerator for 3 to 5 (

VARIATION: Add more spices for pizazz, like ground cumin or cinnamon. You can also use brown rice or quinoa in place of the bulgur.

Per serving: Calories: 550; Total fat: 20g; Carbohydrates: 82g; Fiber: 21g; Protein: 15g; Calcium: 157mg; Vitamin D: 0mcg; Vitamin B$_{12}$: 0mcg; Iron: 4mg; Zinc: <1mg

Sweet Beet Grain Bowl

Serves 2 / Prep time: 10 minutes / Cook time: 20 minutes
HIGH-FIBER, ONE POT, VEGETARIAN

If you're not a beet person, you probably just haven't found the perfect preparation or the right variety of beet. Beets can be pickled, roasted, boiled, shaved raw into salads, pureed into soup or sauce, and even baked into bread. There are also many varieties to choose from, such as candy-cane-striped Chioggia, golden, red, and white (aka sugar beets), just to name a few. There is undoubtedly a beet for you. Here is a recipe that will surely get you hooked on these sweet, earthy, gorgeous root vegetables.

3 cups water

1 cup farro, rinsed

2 tablespoons extra-virgin olive oil

1 tablespoon honey

3 tablespoons cider vinegar

Pinch freshly ground black pepper

4 small cooked beets, sliced

1 pear, cored and diced

6 cups mixed greens

⅓ cup pumpkin seeds, roasted

¼ cup ricotta cheese

1. In a medium saucepan, stir together the water and farro over high heat a bring to a boil. Reduce the heat to medium and simmer until the farro is tender, 15 to 20 minutes. Drain and rinse the farro under cold running v until cool. Set aside.

2. Meanwhile, in a small bowl, whisk together the extra-virgin olive oil, ho and vinegar. Season with black pepper.

3. Evenly divide the farro between two bowls. Top each with the beets, pea greens, pumpkin seeds, and ricotta. Drizzle the bowls with the dressing

before serving and adjust the seasonings as desired.

VARIATION: This recipe can be modified to include vegetables and fruits you may have on hand at home, such as carrots or parsnips. Also, you can swap out the grain for another type or add beans or lentils for more protein. This salad is an easy way to get nourished without having to think about it too hard.

MAKE IT EASIER: You can sometimes purchase cooked beets at the grocery store, saving you from needing to roast them at home.

Per serving: Calories: 779; Total fat: 29g; Carbohydrates: 108g; Fiber: 15g; Protein: 26g; Calcium: 212mg; Vitamin D: <1mcg; Vitamin B$_{12}$: <1mcg; Iron: 8mg; Zinc: 2mg

Grilled Romaine with White Beans

Serves 4 to 6 / Prep time: 5 minutes / Cook time: 8 minutes
GLUTEN-FREE, HIGH-FIBER, VEGETARIAN

When people think of romaine, they often only picture it in salad form—chilled, dressed, maybe with a couple of croutons. Romaine on the grill is, arguably, the better way to enjoy it, and the complexity of the miso makes this plate all the more enjoyable. Miso is a Japanese seasoning paste that can be found in Asian markets but is also widely available at grocery stores. It takes years for the miso to age and finish fermenting, and this process creates a one-of-a-kind, intensely flavorful ingredient.

3 tablespoons extra-virgin olive oil, divided

2 large heads romaine lettuce, halved lengthwise

2 tablespoons white miso

1 tablespoon water, plus more as needed

1 (15-ounce) can white beans, rinsed and drained

½ cup chopped fresh parsley

1. Preheat the grill or a grill pan.

2. Drizzle 2 tablespoons of extra-virgin olive oil over the cut sides of the romaine lettuce.

3. In a medium bowl, whisk the remaining 1 tablespoon of extra-virgin oliv with the white miso and about 1 tablespoon of water. Add more water, if necessary, to reach a thin consistency. Add the white beans and parsley bowl, stir, adjust the seasonings as desired, and set aside.

4. When the grill is hot, put the romaine on the grill and cook for 1 to 2 mir on each side or until lightly charred with grill marks. Remove the lettuce the grill and repeat with remaining lettuce halves. Set the lettuce aside platter or individual plates and top with the beans.

5. Serve.

SUBSTITUTION TIP: If you decide not to add the miso, I recommend squeezing fresh citrus or using vinegar to help replace some of the zing.

Per serving: Calories: 291; Total fat: 12g; Carbohydrates: 38g; Fiber: 14g; Protein: 14g; Calcium: 197mg; Vitamin D: 0mcg; Vitamin B_{12}: 0mcg; Iron: 8mg; Zinc: 2mg

Chickpea Fattoush Salad

Serves 4 / Prep time: 15 minutes / Cook time: 5 minutes
HIGH-FIBER, VEGETARIAN

Panzanella is a Tuscan salad featuring tomatoes, onions, and heaps of stale bread cubes dressed with simple oil and vinegar. It is a lovely summer salad. Fattoush is the Levantine version of this Italian classic. Instead of bread, Fattoush uses toasted pita, chickpeas, and an assortment of mixed greens and vegetables. This recipe offers a similarly delectable salad to panzanella without nearly as many carbs.

2 tablespoons extra-virgin olive oil

2 pitas, torn into bite-size pieces

1 (15-ounce) can chickpeas, rinsed and drained

1 head romaine lettuce, cut into bite-size pieces

1 cucumber, diced

½ pint cherry tomatoes, halved

8 radishes, thinly sliced

1 bunch fresh parsley, chopped

1 cup mint, chopped

½ teaspoon sumac (optional)

½ cup <u>Lemon Vinaigrette Dressing</u> **or store-bought**

1. Heat the extra-virgin olive oil in a large skillet over medium-high heat a sauté the pita bread until toasted and crisp, about 3 minutes. Remove th skillet from the heat and transfer the pita bread to a medium bowl.

2. Add the chickpeas, romaine, cucumber, tomatoes, radishes, parsley, mir sumac (if using) to the medium bowl. Add the dressing and toss to comb Serve.

3. Store any leftovers in an airtight container in the refrigerator for up to ?

Per serving: Calories: 466; Total fat: 30g; Carbohydrates: 42g; Fiber: 10g; Protein: 11g; Calcium: 159mg; Vitamin D: 0mcg; Vitamin B_{12}: 0mcg; Iron: 5mg; Zinc: 1mg

Roasted Carrot and Quinoa with Goat Cheese

Serves 4 / Prep time: 10 minutes / Cook time: 20 minutes
GLUTEN-FREE, HIGH-FIBER, VEGETARIAN

Think of the warmth of long, lazy summer nights and the tantalizing scent of vegetables roasting. Then think of fresh, tart goat cheese with hearty, chewy grains. You just conjured up this delightful salad. Roasted carrots pair magnificently with the earthy qualities of quinoa and creamy goat cheese—this is one of those addictingly delicious salads that is full of nutrition and celebrates the natural flavors that come from the land.

4 large carrots, cut into ⅛-inch-thick rounds

4 tablespoons oil (olive, safflower, or grapeseed), divided

2 teaspoons paprika

1 teaspoon turmeric

2 teaspoons ground cumin

2 cups water

1 cup quinoa, rinsed

½ cup shelled pistachios, toasted

4 ounces goat cheese

12 ounces salad greens

1. Preheat the oven to 400°F. Line a baking sheet with parchment paper.

2. In a large bowl, toss together the carrots, 2 tablespoons of oil, the paprik turmeric, and cumin until the carrots are well coated. Spread them ever the prepared baking sheet and roast until tender, 15 to 17 minutes.

3. In a medium saucepan, combine the water and quinoa over high heat. B to a boil, reduce the heat to low and simmer until tender, about 15 minu

4. Transfer the roasted carrots to a large bowl and add the cooked quinoa, remaining 2 tablespoons of oil, the pistachios, and goat cheese and toss combine.

5. Evenly divide the greens among four plates and top with the carrot mix
   Serve.

6. Store any leftovers in an airtight container in the refrigerator for up to 2

VARIATION: If it's summer, grill the carrots instead and consider serving the salad over plain Greek yogurt for a creamy, unique taste and texture sensation.

Per serving: Calories: 527; Total fat: 31g; Carbohydrates: 48g; Fiber: 10g; Protein: 17g; Calcium: 197mg; Vitamin D: <1mcg; Vitamin B_{12}: <1mcg; Iron: 5mg; Zinc: <1mg

Turkey Pastrami and Pimento Cheese Sandwich

CHAPTER FIVE
Sandwiches and Soups

Who doesn't love a good sandwich? Sometimes it can be challenging to make sandwiches that are lower in carbohydrates. These recipes demonstrate how you can cut back on the carbs and still enjoy bread. Look for sandwich thins or flatbreads, and serve sandwiches as open-faced or tucked into lettuce leaves. Many breads are available in gluten-free varieties with the addition of vegetables such as cauliflower or spinach—or you can procure coconut wraps for your recipes.

What would a sandwich chapter be without soup, the best companion to this creation? Some soups in this section are good stand-alones; others pair beautifully with sandwiches. My suggestion is to eat less of each so that you can enjoy both.

I

Roasted Tomato Tartine

Cauli-Lettuce Wraps

Miso, Tempeh, and Carrot Wraps

Chicken Salad with Apricots

Smoked Salmon on Toast

Red Lentil Sloppy Joes with Roasted Asparagus

Turkey Pastrami and Pimento Cheese Sandwich

Game-Day Burger with Jicama Chips

Minted Sweet Pea Soup

Egg Drop Soup

Tomato-Basil Soup with Grilled Cheese Croutons

West African–Inspired Peanut Soup

Chickpea Spinach Soup

Golden Chicken Soup

Smoked Turkey Chili

Quick Moroccan-Inspired Chicken Stew

Roasted Tomato Tartine

Serves 2 / Prep time: 5 minutes / Cook time: 15 minutes
HIGH-FIBER, VEGETARIAN

Less bread, more tomato is the equation for this delicious sandwich. This recipe goes to show that you don't have to remove bread entirely from your diet; instead, just don't eat as much. Flavorful whole-grain bread acts as a vehicle here for vibrant tomatoes, fresh basil, and tart balsamic vinegar. I like sprouted rye bread with this. If you want to add more seasonings or fresh herbs, it's up to you.

3 tomatoes, cut into eighths

2 tablespoons extra-virgin olive oil, divided

1 tablespoon balsamic vinegar

2 garlic cloves, minced

Pinch kosher salt

Pinch freshly ground black pepper

½ cup ricotta cheese

2 slices whole-grain bread

2 tablespoons chopped fresh basil

4 cups arugula

1. Preheat the oven to 450°F. Line a baking sheet with parchment paper.

2. In a medium-size bowl, toss the tomatoes with 1 tablespoon of extra-vir olive oil, the vinegar, garlic, salt, and pepper.

3. Spread the tomatoes on the baking sheet and bake for 15 minutes.

4. Meanwhile, place the ricotta in the bowl of a food processor and, while i running, add the remaining 1 tablespoon of extra-virgin olive oil in a thi stream. Pause to scrape down the sides if needed. Taste and adjust the seasonings as needed. If you do not have a food processor, whisk the ric(and extra-virgin olive oil in a medium bowl.

5. Toast the bread and divide the ricotta between the slices, spreading it ou evenly. Top the ricotta with the tomatoes and garnish with chopped bas

6. Serve with the greens on the side.

VARIATION: Want more ricotta whip on this sandwich? Double it up on the bread or double it anyway and store the extra in the refrigerator for up to 1 week for other recipes. Adjust the seasonings with freshly ground black pepper for an even better flavor.

Per serving: Calories: 375; Total fat: 22g; Carbohydrates: 34g; Fiber: 6g; Protein: 13g; Calcium: 291mg; Vitamin D: <1mcg; Vitamin B$_{12}$: 1mcg; Iron: 3mg; Zinc: 2mg

Cauli-Lettuce Wraps

Serves 2 to 4 / Prep time: 10 minutes / Cook time: 20 minutes
HIGH-FIBER, ONE POT, VEGETARIAN

This is a low-calorie, low-carbohydrate meal that will leave your body feeling refreshed and light. With lots of flavor and crunch, it makes for a satisfying meal that's just what the dietitian ordered to keep your blood sugars on track.

1½ **tablespoons sesame oil**

½ **yellow onion, chopped**

8 **ounces mushrooms, thinly sliced**

4 **garlic cloves, minced**

1½ **tablespoons low-sodium soy sauce or tamari**

4 **teaspoons rice wine vinegar**

5 **ounces water chestnuts, drained and liquid reserved**

2½ **cups** Cauliflower Rice

½ **cup coarsely chopped cashews**

4 **large green leaf lettuce leaves**

2 **scallions, both white and green parts, thinly sliced** (optional)

1 **cup chopped cilantro** (optional)

1. Heat the sesame oil in a large skillet over medium heat and sauté the on until translucent, about 3 minutes. Add the mushrooms, garlic, tamari, vinegar, and water chestnuts to the skillet. Cover the skillet with a lid an cook until the mushrooms are softened, about 5 minutes.

2. Add the cauliflower and cashews and mix well. Cover the skillet and coo 2 minutes.

3. Adjust the seasonings as desired and evenly divide the cauliflower mixtu among the lettuce leaves.

4. Serve garnished with scallions (if using) and cilantro (if using).

5. Store any leftovers in an airtight container in the refrigerator for up to 2

INGREDIENT TIP: You can use either tamari or soy sauce here, depending on your preference; they have slightly different flavor profiles largely due to the presence of wheat.

SUBSTITUTION TIP: Use white vinegar or mirin if you can't find rice wine vinegar. Add a fresh chile or some chile oil if you're wanting something spicy.

Per serving: Calories: 413; Total fat: 25g; Carbohydrates: 38g; Fiber: 9g; Protein: 17g; Calcium: 115mg; Vitamin D: <1mcg; Vitamin B_{12}: <1mcg; Iron: 4mg; Zinc: 3mg

Miso, Tempeh, and Carrot Wraps

Serves 1 / Prep time: 10 minutes / Cook time: 10 minutes
GLUTEN-FREE, HIGH-FIBER, VEGETARIAN

Tempeh is a fermented soy product that I use in place of animal protein. It's a wonderful, meaty protein with tons of nutritional benefits and it deserves a place in your refrigerator, especially if you're sick of using tofu. If you don't have tempeh on hand, you can substitute a couple pieces of turkey bacon or shredded cooked chicken for these light and tasty wraps.

2 collard green leaves, washed

½ cup shredded carrots

1 teaspoon grated ginger (optional)

½ tablespoon white or yellow miso

½ tablespoon rice vinegar

½ tablespoon sesame oil

Nonstick cooking oil spray

4 ounces smoky tempeh, sliced

1 cup bean sprouts

4 radishes, thinly sliced

1. Fill a large saucepan three-quarters full of water and bring it to a boil ov high heat. Blanch the collard greens for 3 minutes, remove them from tl water, and cool immediately under cold running water. Allow to dry and with a towel to remove excess water.

2. In a medium bowl, combine the carrots, ginger (if using), miso, vinegar, sesame oil until well mixed.

3. Lightly grease a large skillet with cooking spray and heat it over mediun Panfry the tempeh slices until crispy on each side, about 2 minutes per ?

4. Place the collard greens on a clean work surface and evenly divide the c? mixture, tempeh, bean sprouts, and radishes between them. Fold over tl

of each leaf, tuck one side under, and roll like a burrito. Serve.

5. Store any leftovers in an airtight container in the refrigerator for up to 2

INGREDIENT SWAP: If you want to skip the collard wraps, you could use two (6-inch) corn tortillas instead. Keep in mind that the carbohydrates will double, so consider this recipe two servings instead of one to keep the carbs low.

Per serving: Calories: 396; Total fat: 22g; Carbohydrates: 19g; Fiber: 6g; Protein: 31 g; Calcium: 126mg; Vitamin D: 0mcg; Vitamin B$_{12}$: <1mcg; Iron: 2mg; Zinc: 1mg

Chicken Salad with Apricots

Makes 4 cups / Prep time: 10 minutes
GLUTEN-FREE, NO-COOK, ONE BOWL

Chicken salad, a staple of delis everywhere, doesn't have to be a bland, pale lunch staple. In fact, it becomes one of the more exciting sandwiches on our list with just a little extra spice. Dijon mustard? Sure. Coriander? Why not? And with the addition of toasted almond, parsley, lemon, and dried apricot, this filling becomes something exceptional. If you do not have cooked rotisserie chicken available, substitute canned poultry or tuna.

1 cup plain Greek yogurt

2 tablespoons minced shallots

1 teaspoon ground coriander

1 teaspoon Dijon mustard (optional)

1 tablespoon freshly squeezed lemon juice

¼ teaspoon cayenne pepper   ·

12 ounces cooked rotisserie chicken, shredded

2 cups chopped celery with the leaves

¼ cup slivered almonds, toasted

¼ cup thinly sliced dried apricots

1 bunch fresh parsley, chopped

1. In a medium bowl, mix together the Greek yogurt, shallots, coriander, mustard (if using), lemon juice, and cayenne until well combined.

2. Add the chicken, celery, almonds, apricots, and parsley.

3. Serve on your food of choice (lettuce, crackers, jicama slices, radish slice you name it).

4. Store any leftovers in an airtight container in the refrigerator for up to ⁣

VARIATION: Any dried fruit can be used in place of the apricots, such as blueberries, cranberries, pineapple, mango, or golden raisins. Each will add a lovely chewy texture and balancing sweetness to the filling.

Per 1-cup serving: Calories: 288; Total fat: 16g; Carbohydrates: 12g; Fiber: 3g; Protein: 25g; Calcium: 135mg; Vitamin D: 0mcg; Vitamin B$_{12}$: <1mcg; Iron: 3mg; Zinc: 1mg

Smoked Salmon on Toast

Serves 4 / Prep time: 10 minutes
NO-COOK

This is a classic combination for a reason, and you won't have to travel all the way to the delis of New York City to get it. Pumpernickel bread is exceptional with this recipe, but any whole-grain variety works as well. Sometimes the bread might be labeled differently, but any rye-based, thick brown bread will be fabulous. Since you're trying to cut down on your carbohydrate intake, the bread you choose to enjoy should, of course, be of the highest quality.

FOR THE CREAM CHEESE SPREAD

4 ounces cream cheese

Juice of 1 lemon

1 teaspoon stone-ground mustard

FOR THE SANDWICH

4 slices whole-grain bread

8 ounces smoked salmon

4 radishes, thinly sliced

1 teaspoon capers, rinsed and dried (optional)

¼ cup chopped fresh dill

1 medium cucumber, sliced

TO MAKE THE CREAM CHEESE SPREAD

1. In a small bowl, combine the cream cheese, 1 teaspoon of lemon juice, a mustard. Cream together evenly and add more lemon juice if it's too thi You should be able to spread it on a slice of bread easily.

TO MAKE THE SANDWICH

2. Spread the cream cheese mixture on each slice of bread and top with the salmon, radish slices, capers (if using), and fresh dill.

3. Serve with cucumber slices on the side.

VARIATION: Substitute any cured or smoked fish such as trout, and if you really don't like fish, try cooked, thinly sliced roast beef. Beef, pumpernickel, and cream cheese are a stellar combination.

Per serving: Calories: 287; Total fat: 14g; Carbohydrates: 23g; Fiber: 3g; Protein: 18g; Calcium: 115mg; Vitamin D: 1mcg; Vitamin B_{12}: 2mcg; Iron: 2mg; Zinc: 1mg

Red Lentil Sloppy Joes with Roasted Asparagus

Serves 2 / Prep time: 8 minutes / Cook time: 20 minutes
HIGH-FIBER, VEGETARIAN

This recipe is a modern take on the American classic with healthier lentils in place of ground beef. You can use sandwich thins, cauliflower thins, or serve the tasty filling open-faced; there are countless options to choose from to cut carbs. Keep it to one serving of carbohydrates, 15 grams per serving, if using the bread option, or use lettuce instead to keep those carbs in check.

1 bunch asparagus, woody ends removed

1 tablespoon extra-virgin olive oil, divided

½ cup chopped onion

2 teaspoons chopped serrano pepper (optional)

2 garlic cloves, minced

1½ cups water

½ cup red lentils, rinsed

2 tablespoons ketchup

1 teaspoon paprika

1 sandwich thin or other bread option

1. Preheat the oven to 450°F. Line a baking sheet with parchment paper.

2. In a small bowl, toss the asparagus with 1½ teaspoons of extra-virgin ol until well coated, and spread the vegetables on the prepared baking she Bake for 12 to 15 minutes.

3. Meanwhile, heat the remaining 1½ teaspoons of extra-virgin olive oil in medium saucepan over medium heat and sauté the onion and pepper (if using) until soft and translucent, 2 to 3 minutes. Add the garlic and cool minute.

4. Add the water and lentils and bring to a boil. Reduce the heat to low and simmer, stirring occasionally, until the lentils are tender but not falling

about 10 minutes.

5. Add the ketchup and paprika. Adjust seasonings as desired and allow the mixture to thicken over the heat for a couple of minutes.

6. Serve on a sandwich thin or slice of bread with a side of roasted asparagu

7. Store any leftover filling in an airtight container in the refrigerator for u days.

MAKE IT EASIER: Serve with an assortment of raw veggies if you prefer to skip the asparagus.

Per serving: Calories: 370; Total fat: 9g; Carbohydrates: 61g; Fiber: 14g; Protein: 20g; Calcium: 129mg; Vitamin D: 0mcg; Vitamin B$_{12}$: <1mcg; Iron: 10mg; Zinc: 4mg

Turkey Pastrami and Pimento Cheese Sandwich

Serves 2 / Prep time: 5 minutes
NO-COOK, ONE BOWL

The American South adopted pimento cheese, also called pimiento, depending on who you ask, over the last century, and made it their own. We use it here served with a leaner animal protein, turkey, for a sandwich that is so good it feels a bit like a cheat. The homemade pimento cheese tastes deliciously rich but is a healthier alternative to store-bought products.

FOR THE PIMENTO CHEESE (ENOUGH FOR 4 SANDWICHES)

6 ounces sharp cheddar cheese, shredded

3 tablespoons cream cheese, softened

1 tablespoon plain Greek yogurt

2 teaspoons diced pimentos

FOR THE TURKEY PASTRAMI SANDWICH

4 ounces Pimento Cheese

4 slices marble rye bread

6 ounces low-sodium turkey pastrami or peppered turkey

4 lettuce leaves

1 red bell pepper, cut into strips

TO MAKE THE PIMENTO CHEESE

1. In a medium bowl, cream together the cheddar, cream cheese, and yogu using a spoon.

2. Add the pimentos and stir to combine. If it's too thick, add a bit of water pimento juice.

TO MAKE THE TURKEY PASTRAMI SANDWICH

3. Spread the pimento cheese on each slice of marble rye bread. Layer the turkey pastrami and lettuce on the cheese spread on two of the bread sli

Place the other two slices of bread, cheese-side down, on the fillings, cre the sandwich.

4. Serve the sandwiches accompanied by sliced red bell pepper.

Per serving: Calories: 510; Total fat: 25g; Carbohydrates: 37g; Fiber: 4g; Protein: 31g; Calcium: 427mg; Vitamin D: <1mcg; Vitamin B_{12}: <1mcg; Iron: 6mg; Zinc: 2mg

Game-Day Burger with Jicama Chips

Serves 2 / Prep time: 5 minutes / Cook time: 22 minutes
HIGH-FIBER

Jicama is an edible root vegetable native to Mexico, which is commonly eaten raw. It has a wonderful crunch that is reminiscent of chips—somewhere between a potato chip and a carrot stick might be the best way to describe it. And when you need something healthy and addictive alongside your burger, it is an inspired choice. After trying these lime-and-chili spiked chips, you might forget all about french fries for good.

¼ **pound ground bison**

¼ **pound ground beef**

½ **teaspoon garlic powder**

½ **teaspoon onion powder**

½ **teaspoon extra-virgin olive oil**

1 small jicama, peeled

Juice of 1 lime

Chili powder (optional)

Bun (optional)

1 tomato, thinly sliced

4 lettuce leaves

OPTIONAL TOPPINGS
Other burger toppings (cheese, onions, mushrooms, etc.)

1. Preheat a grill to medium-high heat.

2. In a large bowl, combine the bison, beef, garlic powder, and onion powd until mixed well. Do not overhandle, squeeze, or compress the meat.

3. Divide the meat into two equal pieces and form each into a patty.

4. Lightly oil both sides of the burger to prevent sticking and grill on the fi[r] side for 5 to 6 minutes, or until juices start to come through. Turn once [a] grill on the other side for another 5 to 6 minutes, or until the internal temperature is 160°F. If you want to add cheese, layer on a slice during t[he] last minute.

5. If you do not have a grill, heat a grill pan or cast-iron skillet with 1 tables[poon] of oil over medium-high heat and cook the burgers, turning once, until t[hey] reach the correct internal temperature, about 14 minutes in total.

6. Let the burgers rest 5 to 10 minutes, so the juices settle, then add the de[sired] toppings.

7. Meanwhile, slice the jicama into ¼-inch-thick slices, then into quarter[s]. the jicama in a medium bowl and add the lime juice and chili powder (if using) to taste.

8. Serve the burgers on a bun, or wrapped in lettuce if you're watching car[bs] with your favorite toppings and a side of jicama.

SUBSTITUTION TIP: If you can't get bison, substitute any ground meat such as pork, turkey, lamb, chicken, or more beef.

Per serving: Calories: 348; Total fat: 15g; Carbohydrates: 23g; Fiber: 11g; Protein: 32g; Calcium: 69mg; Vitamin D: 0mcg; Vitamin B_{12}: 3mcg; Iron: 5mg; Zinc: 7mg

Minted Sweet Pea Soup

Serves 2 to 4 / Prep time: 10 minutes / Cook time: 10 minutes
GLUTEN-FREE, HIGH-FIBER, VEGETARIAN

I originally discovered this versatile soup recipe when looking for something refreshing to serve. I realized that peas lend themselves well to being chilled, and the addition of the mint makes for a palate-stimulating blend. This soup is just as good hot if you haven't warmed up to the idea of eating cold soup. It is an excellent side for a veggie-packed turkey sandwich or the Asparagus Salad.

2 tablespoons extra-virgin olive oil

1 small yellow onion, minced

Pinch kosher salt

Pinch freshly ground black pepper

2 garlic cloves, minced

1 zucchini, diced

4 cups low-sodium vegetable broth

3 cups frozen peas

Juice of 1 lemon

½ cup plain Greek yogurt (optional)

½ cup thinly sliced fresh mint

2 tablespoons chopped pistachios (optional)

1. Heat the extra-virgin olive oil in a medium stockpot over medium heat. the onion, salt, and pepper and sauté until translucent.

2. Add the garlic and zucchini and sauté until tender, about 3 minutes.

3. Transfer the vegetables to a blender and puree them with the vegetable peas, and lemon juice.

4. Adjust the seasonings as desired and serve the soup warmed in a saucep over medium heat or cooled in the refrigerator. To cool it in an ice bath,

transfer the soup to a medium bowl and nestle that in a large bowl filled ice water.

5. Serve with a dollop of optional Greek yogurt (if using) and topped with 1 and pistachios (if using).

6. Store the cooled soup in an airtight container in the refrigerator for up 1 days, with garnishes kept separately.

SUBSTITUTION TIP: If you don't have vegetable broth on hand, you can use water.

Per serving: Calories: 345; Total fat: 15g; Carbohydrates: 42g; Fiber: 13g; Protein: 12g; Calcium: 115mg; Vitamin D: 0 mcg; Vitamin B_{12}: 0mcg; Iron: 4mg; Zinc: 2mg

Egg Drop Soup

Serves 4 / Prep time: 10 minutes / Cook time: 15 minutes
ONE POT, VEGETARIAN

Egg drop soup has long been a staple of Chinese buffets in the United States. This flavor-packed soup, with its whisper-thin strands of egg and light crunch of scallion, was always my childhood favorite. It is still one of my favorite cold-weather dishes, and I pay homage to those fond memories here.

3½ cups low-sodium vegetable broth, divided

1 teaspoon grated fresh ginger (optional)

2 garlic cloves, minced

3 teaspoons low-sodium soy sauce or tamari

1 tablespoon cornstarch

2 large eggs, lightly beaten

2 scallions, both white and green parts, thinly sliced

1. In a large saucepan, bring 3 cups plus 6 tablespoons of vegetable broth a the ginger (if using), garlic, and tamari to a boil over medium-high heat.

2. In a small bowl, make a slurry by combining the cornstarch and the remaining 2 tablespoons of broth. Stir until dissolved. Slowly add the cornstarch mixture to the rest of the heated soup, stirring until thicken to 3 minutes.

3. Reduce the heat to low and simmer. While stirring the soup, pour the eg slowly. Turn off the heat, add the scallions, and serve.

4. Store the cooled soup in an airtight container in the refrigerator for up 1 days.

INGREDIENT TIP: Look for no-sodium or low-sodium soy sauce or tamari for this soup. Both sauces are typically high in sodium, but if you want to reduce your intake, add half the recommended amount in the recipe. Use tamari to make this recipe gluten-free.

Per serving: Calories: 66; Total fat: 3g; Carbohydrates: 6g; Fiber: 1g; Protein: 4g;
Calcium: 40mg; Vitamin D: 1mcg; Vitamin B_{12}: <1mcg; Iron: 1mg; Zinc: <1mg

Tomato-Basil Soup with Grilled Cheese Croutons

Serves 4 to 6 / Prep time: 10 minutes / Cook time: 20 minutes
GLUTEN-FREE (SOUP ONLY), HIGH FIBER, VEGETARIAN

Tomato soup does not have to be the pale, bland canned version; it can be vibrant and bursting with summer flavor and bright color. Fresh tomatoes are ideal for this recipe when they're in season during the summer and autumn, but there's nothing wrong with canned. Outside of this harvest time frame, fresh tomatoes tend to be mealy and mushy. If you are trying to cut down on calories, use cooking spray instead of butter to make the croutons. Make your own spray by filling a spray bottle with oil to avoid the preservatives in store-bought products.

FOR THE TOMATO SOUP

2 tablespoons extra-virgin olive oil

1 onion, chopped

1 tablespoon minced garlic

3 pounds fresh tomatoes, cored and chopped, or canned diced tomatoes

8 cups low-sodium vegetable broth

4 tablespoons tomato paste

½ cup coconut milk

½ teaspoon garlic powder

Pinch kosher salt

Pinch freshly ground black pepper

⅓ cup fresh basil, chopped

FOR THE GRILLED CHEESE CROUTONS

1 tablespoon butter or cooking spray

4 slices whole-wheat bread

4 ounces cheese (cheddar or Gruyère), shredded

Freshly ground black pepper (optional)

TO MAKE THE TOMATO SOUP

1. Heat the extra-virgin olive oil in a medium stockpot over medium heat. the onion and minced garlic until translucent, about 3 minutes.

2. Add the tomatoes and vegetable broth, increase the heat to medium-hig cover, and simmer until the tomato skin wrinkles and pulls back from tl tomato flesh, 8 to 10 minutes.

3. Add the tomato paste, coconut milk, garlic powder, salt, and pepper and simmer for 3 to 5 minutes.

4. Transfer the soup to a blender and blend until smooth, in batches if necessary. Leave the center piece out of the lid and cover the lid with a c kitchen towel while blending to allow the steam to escape.

5. Pour the soup back into the stockpot.

6. Serve the soup topped with basil and the grilled cheese croutons (if usin

7. Store the cooled soup in an airtight container in the refrigerator for 3 to days. Keep the garnishes separate.

TO MAKE THE GRILLED CHEESE CROUTONS

8. Meanwhile, apply the butter on one side of each slice of bread.

9. Put a small nonstick skillet over medium heat, and place 1 slice of bread skillet, buttered-side down. Top with half of the cheese and season with pepper (if using). Then top with the second slice of bread, buttered-side When the underside is golden brown, 3 to 4 minutes, turn the sandwich until the second side of the bread is golden and crispy.

10. Repeat with the remaining ingredients.

11. Cut each sandwich into 1-inch squares and use them to garnish the soup

MAKE IT EASIER: If you want to cut down on carbohydrates but still want the grilled cheese, use half the bread, cube it into ¼-inch-square pieces, and brown them in a skillet with 1 teaspoon of extra-virgin olive oil or fat. Sprinkle the cubes on the tomato soup followed by the shredded cheese.

Per serving: Calories: 230; Total fat: 13g; Carbohydrates: 27g; Fiber: 7g; Protein: 4g; Calcium: 87mg; Vitamin D: 0mcg; Vitamin B$_{12}$: 0mcg; Iron: 2mg; Zinc: 1mg

West African–Inspired Peanut Soup

Serves 4 to 6 / Prep time: 10 minutes / Cook time: 20 minutes
GLUTEN-FREE, HIGH-FIBER, ONE-POT, VEGETARIAN

This soup has a complex, spicy taste and creamy, rich texture from peanut butter and coconut milk. If you are sensitive to spice, you can adjust the soup to suit your palate by removing some or all of the jalapeño seeds before mincing the pepper. Traditionally, this recipe is served over cooked rice. However, if you're trying to limit your rice consumption, use ⅓ cup of brown rice instead of a larger amount.

6 garlic cloves, minced

1½-inch piece ginger, grated

1 jalapeño pepper, stemmed, halved, and minced, divided

Kosher salt

2 (14-ounce) cans coconut milk, divided

2 tablespoons vegetable oil, divided

1 teaspoon turmeric

½ cup unsweetened peanut butter

8 cups vegetable broth

2 sweet potatoes, cut into ½-inch cubes

1 bunch collard greens, chopped

Juice of 1 lime

Freshly ground black pepper

½ cup chopped cilantro

1. Place the garlic, ginger, half the jalapeño, and a pinch of salt in a mound cutting board. Use the flat of your knife to create a paste. The paste can be made in a food processor or with a mortar and pestle.

2. Scoop 3 tablespoons of the solid white coconut fat off the top of one can coconut milk and place it in a large Dutch oven or stockpot. Add 1 tables of vegetable oil to the coconut fat and heat over medium-high heat, stirr frequently, until the coconut fat separates and the solids start to sizzle,

2 minutes. Continue cooking, stirring constantly, until the solids turn p
golden brown, about 1 minute longer. Add the garlic paste, turmeric, an
peanut butter. Cook, stirring, until aromatic, about 30 seconds.

3. Add the remaining coconut milk from both cans, the broth, and sweet
   potatoes. Bring the soup to a boil, reduce the heat to low, and simmer ur
   the sweet potatoes are tender, about 15 minutes.

4. When the potatoes are cooked through, use a large spoon to smash abou
   of the sweet potatoes against the side of the stockpot to help thicken the
   Add the collard greens and lime juice.

5. Season the soup to taste with salt and pepper and serve topped with cila
   and the remaining minced jalapeños.

6. Store the cooled soup in an airtight container in the refrigerator for 3 to
   days.

NUTRIENT BOOST: Want more vegetables in this hearty soup? Double up on the
greens or add more diced yellow onion.

Per serving: Calories: 706; Total fat: 58g; Carbohydrates: 42g; Fiber: 8g; Protein:
13g; Calcium: 180mg; Vitamin D: 0mcg; Vitamin B_{12}: 0mcg; Iron: 3mg; Zinc: 2mg

Chickpea Spinach Soup

Serves 4 / Prep time: 5 minutes / Cook time: 25 minutes
GLUTEN-FREE, HIGH-FIBER, VEGETARIAN

Chickpeas offer a lot of protein—you'll see them pop up more than once in this book—but they're also a fantastic ingredient because they take on the flavor of the other elements in the recipe. The texture of these legumes also combines beautifully with most accompanying ingredients. This soup makes full use of this characteristic. Take the time to enjoy how the various spices come together in this dish and discover the vibrancy of vegetarian soups.

4 medium carrots, cut into ¼-inch pieces

3 tablespoons extra-virgin olive oil, divided

1 teaspoon ground cumin

1 teaspoon paprika

½ teaspoon ground coriander

½ teaspoon ground cinnamon

2 (15-ounce) cans chickpeas, drained and rinsed

1 onion, thinly sliced

2 tablespoons minced fresh ginger

5 cups low-sodium vegetable broth

1 pound fresh baby spinach

1 cup Greek yogurt (optional)

1. Preheat the oven to 425°F. Line a baking sheet with parchment paper.

2. In a medium bowl, toss the carrots with 2 tablespoons of extra-virgin ol the cumin, paprika, coriander, and cinnamon. Spread the carrots evenly the baking sheet and roast for 8 to 10 minutes. Add half the chickpeas to carrots, place the baking sheet back in the oven, and roast until the carr tender, about 10 minutes more. Set aside.

3. Meanwhile, heat the remaining 1 tablespoon of extra-virgin olive oil in a stockpot over medium-high heat. Sauté the onion in the oil until translu

about 3 minutes, then add the ginger, remaining chickpeas, broth, and spinach. Bring the soup to a boil, reduce the heat to low, and simmer un greens begin to wilt, 2 to 3 minutes.

4. Transfer the soup to a blender and puree until smooth. Leave the center out of the lid and cover the lid with a clean dish towel to allow the steam escape. Adjust the seasonings as desired and thin the soup with water or additional broth if you prefer a thinner soup.

5. Divide the soup among four bowls and serve topped with yogurt (if usin the carrot and chickpea topping.

6. Store the cooled soup in an airtight container in the refrigerator for 3 to days.

MAKE IT EASIER: If you have the spice blend ras el hanout, use 3 teaspoons of that in place of all the spices combined (cumin, paprika, coriander, and cinnamon). Sometimes it can be difficult to find, but it's a lovely spice blend.

Per serving: Calories: 344; Total fat: 14g; Carbohydrates: 45g; Fiber: 13g; Protein: 12g; Calcium: 157mg; Vitamin D: 0mcg; Vitamin B$_{12}$: 0mcg; Iron: 3mg; Zinc: 1mg

Golden Chicken Soup

Serves 4 to 6 / Prep time: 10 minutes / Cook time: 20 minutes
GLUTEN-FREE, ONE POT

This recipe gets its name from the turmeric, an ingredient that is a staple in most people's kitchen these days. What's so special about this spice? It contains a component called curcumin that been shown to benefit inflammatory conditions, metabolic syndrome, pain, and kidney health. However, this component does not absorb well in the body unless it is paired with certain foods like black pepper. This soup contains another tasty ingredient, fennel, which has a distinct anise flavor.

1 tablespoon extra-virgin olive oil

1 yellow onion, chopped

2 teaspoons garlic powder

1 tablespoon ginger powder

2 teaspoons turmeric

½ teaspoon freshly ground black pepper

6 cups low-sodium chicken broth

3 (5- to 6-ounce) boneless, skinless chicken breasts

4 celery stalks, cut into ¼-inch-thick slices

1 fennel bulb, thinly sliced

1. Heat the extra-virgin olive oil in a large stockpot over medium heat. Sau onion until translucent, about 3 minutes. Add the garlic powder, ginger powder, turmeric, black pepper, and chicken broth.

2. Bring to a boil, then carefully add the chicken, celery, and fennel. Reduc heat to medium-low, cover, and simmer until the internal temperature chicken is 160°F, 5 to 10 minutes.

3. Remove the chicken breasts and allow them to cool for 5 minutes while soup keeps simmering.

4. Shred the chicken using two forks and return it to the stockpot. Heat the for about 1 minute and adjust the seasonings as desired.

5. Store the cooled soup in an airtight container in the refrigerator for 3 to days.

MAKE IT EASIER: Ground ginger is less flavorful than fresh ginger, but it can be easier to use the ground product. Whichever you have, you can change out one for the other. For every 1 tablespoon of fresh ginger, use ¼ teaspoon of ground ginger.

Per serving: Calories: 218; Total fat: 7g; Carbohydrates: 13g; Fiber: 4g; Protein: 29g; Calcium: 56mg; Vitamin D: 0mcg; Vitamin B$_{12}$: 0mcg; Iron: 3mg; Zinc: <1mg

Smoked Turkey Chili

Serves 4 / Prep time: 10 minutes / Cook time: 20 minutes
GLUTEN-FREE, HIGH-FIBER, ONE POT

Adding cocoa powder to chili was something one of the chef instructors taught me at culinary school. He also loved to add a smoky element to chili, which is why I think the adobo sauce and fire-roasted tomatoes are ideal additions as well. You can use regular canned tomatoes if you have those available instead. Make this chili ahead of time or cook it for longer to allow for a richer, deeper flavor. All good meaty stews develop complex flavor over time.

1 tablespoon extra-virgin olive oil

1 yellow onion, diced

2 bell peppers, diced

½ pound ground turkey

1½ teaspoons ground cumin

1 teaspoon ground coriander

1 tablespoon cocoa powder (optional)

3 tablespoons adobo sauce

1 cup low-sodium chicken or vegetable broth

1 (28-ounce) can crushed fire-roasted tomatoes

2 (15-ounce) cans cooked beans (kidney beans, black beans, or navy beans), rinsed and drained

1. Heat the extra-virgin olive oil in a large stockpot over medium-high hea the onion and bell peppers and sauté until softened, about 5 minutes.

2. Add the ground turkey and sauté until cooked through, 3 to 5 minutes. A the cumin, coriander, cocoa powder (if using), and adobo sauce. Stir wel add the broth, tomatoes, and beans.

3. Bring to a boil, reduce the heat to low, and simmer for at least 15 minute longer you have, the better the flavors will be enhanced. Serve.

4. Store the cooled chili in an airtight container in the refrigerator for 3 to days.

VARIATION: Replace the ground turkey with 1 cup of quinoa or 2 cups cubed of butternut squash and use the vegetable broth if you'd prefer to make this chili vegan. These substitutions will take about 15 minutes to cook and can be added after you've sautéed the onions and vegetables.

Per serving: Calories: 329; Total fat: 12g; Carbohydrates: 37g; Fiber: 13g; Protein: 19g; Calcium: 93mg; Vitamin D: <1mcg; Vitamin B$_{12}$: 1mcg; Iron: 4mg; Zinc: 2mg

Quick Moroccan-Inspired Chicken Stew

Serves 4 to 6 / Prep time: 5 minutes / Cook time: 15 minutes
GLUTEN-FREE, ONE POT

The inspiration behind this recipe comes from a Moroccan cooking class I teach regularly. Traditionally, this recipe is made using a tagine, an earthenware cooking vessel popular in North Africa. You can substitute a Dutch oven or use a large pan with a lid to capture the moisture. This is a sped-up version of the classic recipe. If you have the time, extend the cooking time once all the ingredients are combined to create a rich, deeply flavored stew.

2 teaspoons ground cumin

1 teaspoon ground cinnamon

½ teaspoon turmeric

½ teaspoon paprika

1½ pounds boneless, skinless chicken, cut into strips

2 tablespoons extra-virgin olive oil

5 garlic cloves, smashed and coarsely chopped

2 onions, thinly sliced

1 tablespoon fresh lemon zest

½ cup coarsely chopped olives

2 cups low-sodium chicken broth

Cilantro, for garnish (optional)

1. In a medium bowl, mix together the cumin, cinnamon, turmeric, and pa until well blended. Add the chicken, tossing to coat, and set aside.

2. Heat the extra-virgin olive oil in a large skillet or medium Dutch oven o medium-high heat. Add the chicken and garlic in one layer and cook, browning on all sides, about 2 minutes.

3. Add the onions, lemon zest, olives, and broth and bring the soup to a boi Reduce the heat to medium low, cover, and simmer for 8 minutes.

4. Uncover the soup and let it simmer for another 2 to 3 minutes for the sa thicken slightly. Adjust the seasonings as desired and serve garnished w cilantro (if using).

5. Store the cooled soup in an airtight container in the refrigerator for up 1 days.

VARIATION: Make this stew vegetarian by omitting the chicken and adding cooked chickpeas. Also, swap out the chicken broth for a vegetarian product.

Per serving: Calories: 315; Total fat: 14g; Carbohydrates: 9g; Fiber: 2g; Protein: 40g; Calcium: 55mg; Vitamin D: 0mcg; Vitamin B$_{12}$: 0mcg; Iron: 3mg; Zinc: <1mg

Chicken Sausage and Cauliflower Pizza

CHAPTER SIX
Mains

Our culture reveres big plates and 16-ounce steaks. We've long held the view that large portions are the only prerequisite for being called the main course. While I want to ensure that you remain satiated—no one who follows the recipes in this cookbook will go to bed hungry—this mentality couldn't be further from the truth. Having the *right* items on your plate, as opposed to a mountain of empty calories or extra-large portions, is infinitely more important.

The main courses in this chapter draw inspiration from all over the world and lean into lighter, healthier vegetable replacements for meats. You might be surprised at how many of your favorites can be found in this book. I also draw from the cuisines of other countries and cultures to ensure a balanced diet that incorporates everything you need to expand your horizons while eating healthy to boot.

m

Gingered Red Lentils with Millet

Eggplant and Lentils with Curried Yogurt

Peanut Tofu over Buckwheat Noodles

Simple Bibimbap

Vegetable Mac 'n' Cheese

Jackfruit Tacos

Cauliflower Steaks with Tomato, Caper, and Golden Raisin Sauce

Tuna Poke with Riced Broccoli

Walnut-Crusted Halibut with Pear Salad

Italian-Style Turkey Meatballs and Zoodles

Ribboned Squash with Bacon

Chicken Khao Sen with Rice Noodles

Lebanese-Inspired Beef Kebabs with Pickled Onions

Salmon en Papillote

Cherry Barbecue Chicken Cutlets

Miso Skirt Steak

Herbed Buttermilk Chicken

Chicken Sausage and Cauliflower Pizza

Turkey Bolognese with Chickpea Pasta

Gingered Red Lentils with Millet

Serves 4 / Prep time: 10 minutes / Cook time: 20 minutes
GLUTEN-FREE, HIGH-FIBER, VEGETARIAN

This recipe is inspired by the delicious cuisine of India—where it would be called *dal*. One of my favorite food countries, India, has long ago mastered the art of balanced eating, with the understanding that you don't have to sacrifice great, bold flavors to enjoy vegetarian food. You will find the blend of ginger, mint, onions, and tomato in this dish is, in a word, perfect.

3 cups water

1 cup millet, rinsed

½ cup red lentils, rinsed

3 tablespoons extra-virgin olive oil, divided

Pinch kosher salt

1 onion, diced

3-inch piece ginger, grated (or minced)

4 cups cherry tomatoes, diced

3 tablespoons unsalted peanuts, chopped

2 limes, quartered

1 bunch mint leaves

1. In a medium saucepan over medium heat, stir together the water, millet lentils, 1 tablespoon of extra-virgin olive oil, and the salt. Bring to a boil, reduce the heat to low, cover, and simmer until tender, about 15 minute: Remove the saucepan from the heat and let the grains sit for a few minu

2. Meanwhile, in a small saucepan, heat the remaining 2 tablespoons of ex virgin olive oil. Sauté the onion until translucent, about 3 minutes. Add ginger, tomatoes, and peanuts. Cook for about 5 minutes, adjust the seasonings as desired, and allow to sit until the millet and lentils are fini

3. Divide the millet and lentils among four bowls, and top them with the gingered onion mixture. Garnish with lime wedges and mint leaves.

4. Serve, and store any leftovers in an airtight container in the refrigerator up to 3 days.

MAKE IT EASIER: Only want to cook for two? Simply use half the ingredients or pack up the leftovers in an airtight container in the refrigerator to enjoy another day.

Per serving: Calories: 439; Total fat: 16g; Carbohydrates: 62g; Fiber: 8g; Protein: 15g; Calcium: 46mg; Vitamin D: 0mcg; Vitamin B$_{12}$: 0mcg; Iron: 5mg; Zinc: 1mg

Eggplant and Lentils with Curried Yogurt

Serves 4 / Prep time: 10 minutes / Cook time: 20 minutes
GLUTEN-FREE, HIGH-FIBER, VEGETARIAN

My partner has perfected this flavorful recipe. He can get anyone to eat eggplant when he prepares this dish, and it is definitely a crowd-pleasing recipe that's enjoyed above any other at our friend's potluck dinners. If you have the time before you begin cooking, soaking the lentils for 1 hour before preparing this dish helps shorten the cooking time.

2 large eggplants

4 tablespoons extra-virgin olive oil, divided

Kosher salt

2 cups water

1 cup brown lentils, rinsed and soaked (optional to soak)

1 teaspoon ground cumin, divided

¾ cup plain Greek yogurt

2 teaspoons curry powder

Zest and juice of 1 lime

1 onion, thinly sliced

¼ cup sliced almonds

½ teaspoon ground coriander

¼ cup pomegranate seeds

1. Preheat the oven to 450°F. Line a baking sheet with parchment paper.

2. Use a peeler to peel strips of the skin off of the eggplant lengthwise. Alte strips, leaving some of the purplish-black skin on the eggplant. It shoulc reminiscent of a zebra with the white flesh and dark skin. Cut the peelec eggplant width-wise into ½-inch-thick slices. Place them in a medium l

3. Toss the eggplant with 2 tablespoons of extra-virgin olive oil and a pincl salt. Spread the slices in a single layer on the prepared baking sheet. Roa

eggplant for 20 minutes, until slightly crispy and soft.

4. Meanwhile, in a medium stockpot over medium-high heat, combine the water, lentils, ½ teaspoon of cumin, and a pinch of salt. Bring to a boil, t reduce the heat to low, cover, and simmer for 20 minutes or until the ler are tender. Set aside.

5. In a small bowl, combine the Greek yogurt with the curry powder, a pinc lime zest, and 1 tablespoon of lime juice. Taste and adjust the seasoning: desired. Use the additional lime juice if you feel it should have more citr a looser consistency. Set aside.

6. Heat the remaining 2 tablespoons of extra-virgin olive oil in a medium s over medium-high heat. Sauté the onion until translucent, about 3 minι Add the remaining ½ teaspoon of cumin, the sliced almonds, and coriaι to the skillet, stirring to combine.

7. Arrange the slices of eggplant on four plates, followed by the lentils, spiς yogurt, sautéed onions, and garnish with pomegranate seeds.

SUBSTITUTION TIP: You can use dried cherries or dried cranberries in place of the pomegranate seeds, if preferred.

Per serving: Calories: 479; Total fat: 20g; Carbohydrates: 56g; Fiber: 27g; Protein: 23g; Calcium: 161mg; Vitamin D: 0mcg; Vitamin B_{12}: <1mcg; Iron: 5mg; Zinc: 1mg

Peanut Tofu over Buckwheat Noodles

Serves 2 / Prep time: 5 to 10 minutes / Cook time: 10 minutes
GLUTEN-FREE, HIGH-FIBER, ONE POT, VEGETARIAN

This delightful recipe is loaded with veggies, enough for your entire day, as well as deliciously thick buckwheat noodles. Yes, you can eat noodles if you're a diabetic or are trying to limit your carbohydrates; this recipe simply ensures that you're not getting too much of a good thing.

2 ounces buckwheat noodles

¼ cup <u>Peanut Sauce</u> or store-bought

4 cups shredded cabbage

8 ounces firm tofu, cubed

1 cup diced cucumber

½ cup chopped cilantro

1. Cook the buckwheat noodles according to the package instructions and to cool. This can be done 1 to 2 days in advance, and you can store the co noodles in the refrigerator in an airtight container.

2. In a large bowl, thin the peanut sauce with water if it's too thick. It shou resemble the consistency of a thin dressing. Toss the sauce with the noo cabbage, tofu, cucumber, and cilantro. Adjust the seasonings as desired. Serve.

3. Store any leftovers in an airtight container in the refrigerator for up to ₃

MAKE IT EASIER: If you like extra sauce, double up on the peanut sauce. It will increase your protein and fat to keep you fuller longer.

SUBSTITUTION TIP: If you're not a fan of cilantro, you can use equal amounts of parsley, any lettuce, red cabbage, or shredded carrot instead.

Per serving: Calories: 462; Total fat: 23g; Carbohydrates: 45g; Fiber: 8g; Protein: 26g; Calcium: 277mg; Vitamin D: 0mcg; Vitamin B$_{12}$: 0mcg; Iron: 4mg; Zinc: 1mg

Simple Bibimbap

Serves 2 / Prep time: 15 minutes / Cook time: 15 minutes
HIGH-FIBER, VEGETARIAN

Korean bibimbap ("bibim" means to mix various ingredients and "bap" means rice) is the ultimate casual meal. I've formulated one of my favorite combinations here, but feel free to experiment with the extra veggies and sauces you have in the refrigerator as well. The cauliflower rice helps you cut back on the concentrated carbs of traditional rice, and kimchi is a delicious good-for-your-gut probiotic food that helps with digestion and immunity. You can find it at many grocery stores in the international aisle.

4 teaspoons canola oil, divided

2½ cups Cauliflower Rice

2 cups fresh baby spinach

3 teaspoons low-sodium soy sauce or tamari, divided

8 ounces mushrooms, thinly sliced

2 large eggs

1 cup bean sprouts, rinsed

1 cup kimchi

½ cup shredded carrots

1. Heat 1 teaspoon of canola oil in a medium skillet and sauté the cauliflow rice, spinach, and 2 teaspoons of soy sauce until the greens are wilted, al minutes. Put the vegetables in a small bowl and set aside.

2. Return the skillet to medium heat, add 2 teaspoons of vegetable oil and, it's hot, add the mushrooms in a single layer and cook for 3 to 5 minutes stir and cook another 3 minutes or until mostly golden-brown in color. I the mushrooms in a small bowl and toss them with the remaining 1 teas of soy sauce.

3. Wipe out the skillet and heat the remaining 1 teaspoon of vegetable oil c low heat. Crack in the eggs and cook until the whites are set and the yoll begin to thicken but not harden, 4 to 5 minutes.

4. Assemble two bowls with cauliflower rice and spinach at the bottom. Th
   arrange each ingredient separately around the rim of the bowl: bean spr
   mushrooms, kimchi, and shredded carrots, with the egg placed in the ce
   and serve.

NUTRIENT BOOST: Add some sliced radishes for more vegetables, or serve with whole grains.

Per serving: Calories: 277; Total fat: 15g; Carbohydrates: 20g; Fiber: 8g; Protein: 18g; Calcium: 164mg; Vitamin D: 1mcg; Vitamin B$_{12}$: 1mcg; Iron: 3mg; Zinc: 2mg

Vegetable Mac 'n' Cheese

Serves 2 / Prep time: 10 minutes / Cook time: 20 minutes
HIGH-FIBER, VEGETARIAN

The "comfort food revolution," which introduced items like burgers and tater tots to fine-dining menus all across the country, thankfully also convinced us that macaroni and cheese is not just for children. We limit the pasta shells here and bolster the dish with cauliflower and Brussels sprouts to make this lower-carb and suitable for prediabetes.

2 cups Brussels sprouts, quartered

1 tablespoon extra-virgin olive oil, divided

Pinch kosher salt

Pinch freshly ground black pepper

¼ cup dry whole-wheat pasta shells

½ cup sliced leeks

2 cups small cauliflower florets

4 ounces shredded cheddar cheese

2 tablespoons milk

1. Preheat the oven to 425°F. Line a baking sheet with parchment paper.

2. In a large bowl, toss the Brussels sprouts in 2 teaspoons of extra-virgin oil, the salt, and pepper. Arrange the sprouts on the prepared baking she and roast for 20 minutes, until softened and browned.

3. Meanwhile, bring a medium saucepan filled three-quarters full of water boil over high heat and cook the pasta according to the package instruct Drain and set aside.

4. Heat the remaining 1 teaspoon of extra-virgin olive oil in a medium sauc over medium-high heat and sauté the leeks until translucent, about 3 minutes. Add the cauliflower, cheese, milk, and cooked pasta. Stir until t

mixture has a creamy consistency. Add the Brussels sprouts and toss to combine before serving.

5. Store any leftovers in an airtight container in the refrigerator for up to 4

SUBSTITUTION TIP: Don't let the leeks stop you from making this recipe if you can't find them. Use any onion you'd like as a substitute. You can toss in some kimchi for a Korean take on mac 'n' cheese as well. It's delicious, trust me.

Per serving: Calories: 401; Total fat: 26g; Carbohydrates: 26g; Fiber: 8g; Protein: 21g; Calcium: 481mg; Vitamin D: <1mcg; Vitamin B$_{12}$: <1mcg; Iron: 2mg; Zinc: 1mg

Jackfruit Tacos

Serves 4 / Prep time: 5 minutes / Cook time: 25 minutes
GLUTEN-FREE, HIGH-FIBER, VEGETARIAN

You may have heard of jackfruit as the go-to meat substitute. Not only does it have a succulent, pulled pork–like texture, but it also takes on the flavor and spice of ingredients it's cooked with. Surprisingly, jackfruit is actually best canned as opposed to raw. You can find it in Asian markets or the international aisle of your grocery store.

2 (20-ounce) cans jackfruit in water, rinsed and drained

2 tablespoons extra-virgin olive oil

1 yellow onion, diced

1 cup water

4 garlic cloves, minced

2 teaspoons paprika

1 tablespoon chili powder

1 tablespoon ground cumin

1 chipotle pepper in adobo sauce, minced, plus 2 tablespoons sauce

Juice of 2 limes

OPTIONAL TOPPINGS
Corn tortillas

Shredded cabbage or lettuce

Cheese

Salsa

Cooked beans

Avocado

1. Place the jackfruit in a medium bowl. Sort through it and cut the toughe portion of the jackfruit into smaller pieces. Use your hands to break up of the larger, tender pieces. Pat dry and set aside.

138

2. Heat the extra-virgin olive oil in a large skillet over medium heat and sa
   the onion until translucent, 3 to 5 minutes. Add the jackfruit, water, gar
   paprika, chili powder, cumin, chipotle pepper and adobo sauce, and lime
   juice. Mix well, reduce the heat to medium-low, cover, and cook, stirring
   occasionally, for 15 minutes.

3. Serve with corn tortillas, lettuce or cabbage, and any other taco addition
   see fit.

4. Store any leftovers in an airtight container in the refrigerator for up to 4

VARIATION: Make this recipe a salad by placing the filling components on a bed of fresh
greens or Avocado Slaw.

Per serving: Calories: 139; Total fat: 8g; Carbohydrates: 18g; Fiber: 10g; Protein: 2g;
Calcium: 71mg; Vitamin D: 0mcg; Vitamin B_{12}: 0mcg; Iron: 1mg; Zinc: <1mg

Cauliflower Steaks with Tomato, Caper, and Golden Raisin Sauce

Serves 4 / Prep time: 5 minutes / Cook time: 25 minutes
5-INGREDIENT, GLUTEN-FREE, HIGH FIBER, VEGETARIAN

I was once skeptical about cauliflower steaks as a swap for animal protein, but they're quite delicious! It is the stellar sauce that really makes this dish shine. The combination of tomatoes, capers, and golden raisins with cauliflower creates an Italian-influenced plate that lingers in your memory long after the last bite.

1 large head cauliflower

2 tablespoons extra-virgin olive oil

Pinch kosher salt

Pinch freshly ground black pepper

1 batch <u>Tomato, Caper, and Golden Raisin Sauce</u>

1. Preheat the oven to 400°F. Line a baking sheet with parchment paper.

2. Stand up the cauliflower so that the stem end is flat on the cutting board you hold the crown of the head with your hand. Then, carefully, slice ½ thick "steaks" starting from the crown (top of the head) and moving tow the stem (base). Work from one end to the other. Depending on the size cauliflower, you should get 4 to 6 sliced steaks and some florets.

3. Place the cauliflower steaks and florets on the prepared baking sheet in single layer. Brush them with oil and season with salt and pepper.

4. Roast the cauliflower for 15 minutes until golden brown, then flip the st over and cook for another 10 minutes.

5. To serve, lay the cauliflower steaks on plates and top with the tomato sa

6. Store any leftovers in an airtight container in the refrigerator for up to 4

MAKE IT EASIER: If you really want to cut down on the cooking time, you can always use a canned tomato sauce instead of making the tomato-caper sauce. Simply heat the sauce in a saucepan on the stove until warm.

Per serving: Calories: 275; Total fat: 15g; Carbohydrates: 35g; Fiber: 9g; Protein: 8g; Calcium: 139mg; Vitamin D: 0mcg; Vitamin B$_{12}$: 0mcg; Iron: 4mg; Zinc: 1mg

Tuna Poke with Riced Broccoli

Serves 2 / Prep time: 15 minutes / Cook time: 5 minutes
HIGH-FIBER, ONE PAN

Instead of having rice in your tuna poke bowl, try riced broccoli, your favorite green mini trees. You may be able to find riced broccoli at the store, but it's actually quite easy to prep at home. Simply grate raw broccoli, and that's it! It's loaded with fiber; vitamins C, E, and K; and minerals like folate, calcium, and potassium. It also won't affect your blood sugars like starchy grains. Another option is to use Cauliflower Rice if broccoli isn't an ingredient you're keen on.

FOR THE TUNA POKE

½ pound sushi-grade tuna (see tip), cut into ½-inch cubes

2 tablespoons soy sauce or tamari

1 tablespoon rice vinegar

1 teaspoon sesame oil

FOR THE BOWL

½ tablespoon extra-virgin olive oil

1 small head broccoli, grated

1 cup thawed (if frozen) edamame

1 medium carrot, julienned

1 cucumber, diced

2 scallions, both white and green parts, thinly sliced

OPTIONAL TOPPINGS

Avocado slices

Shaved radish

Toasted sesame seeds

Pickled ginger

TO MAKE THE TUNA POKE

1. In a medium bowl, toss together the tuna, soy sauce, rice vinegar, and se oil.

2. Set aside.

TO MAKE THE BOWL

3. Heat the oil in a large skillet over medium heat and sauté the broccoli u tender, 2 to 3 minutes. Remove the skillet from the heat and allow the broccoli to cool.

4. Assemble two bowls by placing riced broccoli as the base. Top each bowl the tuna poke, edamame, carrot, and cucumber. Drizzle the remaining j from the tuna marinade over the bowls and garnish with sliced scallions

5. Store any leftovers in an airtight container in the refrigerator for up to 2

SUBSTITUTION TIP: Make it a budget tuna poke bowl by using canned tuna instead of fresh. Drain the tuna before adding the seasonings and follow the recipe as instructed.

Per serving: Calories: 374; Total fat: 11g; Carbohydrates: 28g; Fiber: 10g; Protein: 46g; Calcium: 179mg; Vitamin D: 3mcg; Vitamin B_{12}: 0mcg; Iron: 4mg; Zinc: 1mg

Walnut-Crusted Halibut with Pear Salad

Serves 4 / Prep time: 10 minutes / Cook time: 10 minutes
HIGH-FIBER

Halibut is one of my favorite types of whitefish, but another whitefish, such as cod, can be a tasty substitute. Whatever the fish you decide to use, your heart still benefits from the lean protein and healthy fats it has to offer. Additionally, fish is low in carbohydrates and high in protein, especially paired with those non-starchy vegetables you just can't get enough of.

FOR THE HALIBUT

¾ cup finely chopped toasted walnuts

2 tablespoons bread crumbs

¼ cup chopped fresh parsley

2 tablespoons chopped fresh chives

4 (6- to 8-ounce) halibut fillets

Kosher salt

Freshly ground black pepper

1 tablespoon extra-virgin olive oil

FOR THE SALAD

6 cups packed mixed greens

1 pear, thinly sliced

¼ cup chopped fresh parsley

¼ cup chopped fresh chives

Zest and juice of 1 lemon

Extra-virgin olive oil, for the dressing

Kosher salt

Freshly ground black pepper

TO MAKE THE HALIBUT

1. Preheat the broiler. Line a baking sheet with parchment paper.

2. In a small bowl, combine the walnuts, bread crumbs, parsley, and chives

3. Pat the halibut fillets dry, season them with salt and pepper and rub ½ tablespoon of extra-virgin olive oil on each fillet. Place the fillets on the prepared baking sheet. Sprinkle the walnut mixture evenly on top of each fillet and press slightly, so the topping will stick.

4. Broil the fish until the crust is golden and the fish is fully cooked, 5 to 8 minutes.

TO MAKE THE SALAD

5. Meanwhile, in a large bowl, toss the greens, pear, parsley, chives, and zes until well combined. Drizzle the salad with the lemon juice and a bit of e virgin olive oil to taste. Season with salt and pepper to taste.

6. Evenly divide the salad among four plates and top with the fish. Serve.

7. Store any leftovers in an airtight container in the refrigerator for up to 2

NUTRITION BOOST: Serve the fish over a bed of lettuce or salad but keep it simple to show off the fish. Add more vegetables on the side, like the Sautéed Lemon Broccoli and Kale, for a filling meal.

Per serving: Calories: 419; Total fat: 24g; Carbohydrates: 17g; Fiber: 5g; Protein: 37g; Calcium: 81mg; Vitamin D: 6mcg; Vitamin B_{12}: 2mcg; Iron: 3mg; Zinc: 2mg

Italian-Style Turkey Meatballs and Zoodles

Serves 4 / Prep time: 10 minutes / Cook time: 20 minutes
GLUTEN-FREE, HIGH-FIBER

You probably know what zoodles are because this trendy ingredient is in many low-carb recipes. They are spiralized zucchini noodles that take the place of spaghetti or angel hair. Buy zoodles that are already prepared to save time (you can find them in the freezer or produce section). However, if you would like to make them, it's quite easy and something you can do with your kids or with your friends at a group cooking party using a spiralizer. Spiralize one zucchini for each person.

1 pound ground turkey

¼ cup minced onion

4 tablespoons pitted olives (optional)

1 teaspoon dried oregano

1 teaspoon dried thyme

1 teaspoon ground fennel

½ teaspoon kosher salt

1 recipe <u>Basic Marinara</u> or store-bought

8 cups zoodles

Fresh chopped parsley, for garnish

1. Preheat the oven to 375°F. Line a baking sheet with parchment paper.

2. In a large bowl, combine the turkey, onion, olives, oregano, thyme, fenn salt until well mixed. Shape the mixture into 1½-inch meatballs and pla them on the prepared baking sheet. Bake for 15 to 20 minutes until the internal temperature of the meatballs reaches 160°F.

3. Meanwhile, heat the marinara sauce in a large saucepan over medium h Keep the sauce warm until the meatballs are finished cooking.

4. Transfer the meatballs to the sauce and stir to coat.

5. Place 2 cups of zoodles on each plate and top with the marinara sauce and meatballs. Garnish with parsley and serve.

6. Store any leftovers in an airtight container in the refrigerator for up to 4

VARIATION: You can use 2 ounces of whole-wheat noodles in place of the zoodles.

Per serving: Calories: 489; Total fat: 29g; Carbohydrates: 32g; Fiber: 10g; Protein: 25g; Calcium: 103mg; Vitamin D: <1mcg; Vitamin B$_{12}$: 1mcg; Iron: 5mg; Zinc: 3mg

Ribboned Squash with Bacon

Serves 4 / Prep time: 15 minutes / Cook time: 10 minutes
GLUTEN-FREE, HIGH-FIBER

Bacon is not something you need to cut to eat healthfully. This recipe demonstrates how to enjoy bacon in moderation. A single slice of bacon per serving enhances the buttery flavor of the walnuts and sweetness of the squash ribbons. Make the recipe more heart-friendly by omitting the bacon, or vegetarian by swapping out the bacon for cheese or chopped seitan.

¼ **cup dried currants or golden raisins**

¼ **cup red wine vinegar**

1 pound butternut squash, seeded and skin removed

4 bacon slices

2 tablespoons extra-virgin olive oil (optional)

½ **cup chopped, toasted walnuts**

4 cups arugula

Freshly ground black pepper

½ **cup chopped fresh parsley**

1. In a small bowl, combine the currants and vinegar and allow to soak unt tender, about 10 minutes.

2. Using a vegetable peeler, peel the squash into long ribbons into a large b Set aside.

3. Place the bacon slices in a medium skillet over medium heat, cover, and for 8 to 10 minutes until cooked through and crispy. Remove the bacon f the heat and drain it on a paper towel. Chop the bacon into bite-size pie when it's cool enough to handle.

4. Return the pan to medium heat with the bacon fat (or wipe it out and th add the extra-virgin olive oil). Add the walnuts. Heat the walnuts for 2 minutes, then transfer the mixture from the skillet to the squash noodle

toss well. Add the currants with their soaking liquid, along with the arug
and reserved bacon.

5. Season with pepper and serve topped with parsley.

6. Store any leftovers in an airtight container in the refrigerator for up to 4

VARIATION: Mix this simple recipe up with other types of nuts or seeds like almonds, pecans, or pumpkin seeds.

Per serving: Calories: 272; Total fat: 19g; Carbohydrates: 21g; Fiber: 5g; Protein: 7g; Calcium: 106mg; Vitamin D: 0mcg; Vitamin B_{12}: <1mcg; Iron: 2mg; Zinc: 1mg

Chicken Khao Sen with Rice Noodles

Serves 2 / Prep time: 5 to 10 minutes / Cook time: 15 minutes
GLUTEN-FREE, HIGH-FIBER

There is a very large Laotian immigrant population in my hometown, and our local cuisine has become all the better as a result. This recipe for Khao Sen is humbly dedicated to this vibrant slice of the culinary community. Red curry paste and fish sauce can be found in the international or Asian foods aisle. If available, Thai basil and Chinese broccoli will give it an even more authentic flavor.

4 ounces rice noodles

2 tablespoons Thai red curry paste

½ tablespoon fish sauce (optional)

1½ tablespoons extra-virgin olive oil, divided

½ pound ground chicken

1 head broccoli, ends trimmed

½ cup Pickled Red Onions

1 bunch radishes, cut into matchsticks

1 cup bean sprouts

1 tablespoon basil, torn

1 lime, cut into wedges (optional)

1. Bring a large saucepan of water to a boil and cook the rice noodles accor to the package instructions. Rinse well and allow to cool.

2. Heat the curry paste, fish sauce (if using), and 1 tablespoon of extra-virg olive oil in a large skillet over medium-high heat. Add the ground chicke cook thoroughly, about 7 minutes. Set aside in a bowl.

3. Wipe out the skillet and add the remaining ½ tablespoon of extra-virgi oil. Add the broccoli and cook until tender, about 3 minutes.

4. Assemble two bowls with the noodles on the bottom and top them with pickled red onions, cooked chicken, broccoli, radishes, bean sprouts, ba

and a lime wedge (if using, squeeze atop the dish before eating). Serve.

5. Store any leftovers in an airtight container in the refrigerator for up to 4

VARIATION: You can replace the rice noodles in this dish with 1 to 2 cups of zoodles (homemade or store-bought) if you're wanting to reduce total carbs in the dish.

Per serving: Calories: 615; Total fat: 21g; Carbohydrates: 76g; Fiber: 11g; Protein: 34g; Calcium: 182mg; Vitamin D: 0mcg; Vitamin B$_{12}$: 1mcg; Iron: 4mg; Zinc: 4mg

Lebanese-Inspired Beef Kebabs with Pickled Onions

Serves 4 / Prep time: 20 minutes / Cook time: 10 minutes
GLUTEN-FREE

These spiced beef kebabs are both flavorful and healthy. Using a variety of spices can truly eliminate the need for added salt, which is a bonus for your heart. Serve these tender kebabs with curried rice or throw a corn cob on the grill while you're cooking the beef.

1 red bell pepper, chopped

½ onion, coarsely chopped

2 garlic cloves, coarsely chopped

1 pound ground beef

1½ teaspoons ground cumin

1½ teaspoons sumac (optional)

1½ teaspoons red pepper flakes

1 teaspoon kosher salt

Freshly ground black pepper

1 tablespoon ice-cold water

8 (12-inch) metal skewers (or wooden skewers soaked in warm water for 10 to 30 minutes)

1 teaspoon vegetable oil

Pickled Red Onions

1. Place the red pepper, onion, and garlic in a food processor and pulse a fe times until they're very finely chopped but not pureed. Set aside in a bov draining off any excess liquid.

2. Put the beef, processed vegetables, cumin, sumac (if using), red pepper salt, and a pinch of black pepper into the bowl of a stand mixer with the paddle attached. Work on medium speed until the mix starts sticking to sides of the bowl, about a minute. Add the ice-cold water and mix for an

5 minutes, until you have a sticky mass. Chill the meat mixture in the fr
for a few minutes or in the refrigerator for at least 30 minutes (or overn

3. Divide the meat mixture into 8 balls. With a small bowl of cold water be
   you, wet your hands and form the kebab mixture around the skewers,
   distributing it evenly until you have kofta about 9-by-2-inches thick. Sn
   out any holes or tears, then place them on a greaseproof paper–lined ba
   sheet. (Refrigerate the kofta, covered, if you're not cooking them right a

4. Grease a grill pan with the vegetable oil and place it over high heat. Onc
   pan is hot, grill the kofta until charred on the outside and just cooked th
   (adjust the heat as necessary), 8 to 10 minutes. Put the grilled kebabs di
   on top of the pickled red onions on a platter or individual plates, so the j
   drip onto the onions, and serve immediately.

INGREDIENT TIP: Try Aleppo pepper flakes instead of red pepper flakes; they're more authentic to the dish and are available in Middle Eastern grocery stores.

Per serving: Calories: 321; Total fat: 18g; Carbohydrates: 9g; Fiber: 2g; Protein: 31g; Calcium: 49mg; Vitamin D: <1mcg; Vitamin B_{12}: 3mcg; Iron: 4mg; Zinc: 8mg

Salmon en Papillote

Serves 2 / Prep time: 15 minutes / Cook time: 15 minutes
GLUTEN-FREE, HIGH-FIBER

Feeling fancy? En papillote is just French for "baked in paper," a cooking technique that keeps the fish moist and tender. This dish is elegant, delicious, and makes for a fun date-night meal with your sweetheart. You can also use foil instead of parchment and crimp the edges to form a sealed packet.

FOR THE ROASTED VEGETABLES

½ pound fresh green beans, trimmed

½ onion, cut into ¼-inch-thick slices

1 tablespoon extra-virgin olive oil

1 teaspoon capers (optional)

FOR THE SALMON

2 teaspoons extra-virgin olive oil, divided

2 medium parsnips, cut into ¼-inch-thick rounds, divided

2 (4-ounce) salmon fillets

2 garlic cloves, thinly sliced, divided

1 lemon, divided (½ cut into slices, the other ½ cut into 2 wedges)

1 tablespoon chopped fresh thyme, divided

Kosher salt

Freshly ground black pepper

TO MAKE THE ROASTED VEGETABLES

1. Preheat the oven to 400°F. Line a baking sheet with parchment paper.

2. In a medium bowl, toss the green beans, onion, extra-virgin olive oil, and capers (if using) until well coated.

3. Spread the vegetables on half of the baking sheet and set aside until the salmon is ready to bake.

TO MAKE THE SALMON

4. Cut two pieces of parchment paper, fold them in half, and cut each into heart shape (about 10 to 12 inches in circumference). Lightly brush the parchment with ½ teaspoon of extra-virgin olive oil.

5. Open one of the hearts and place half the parsnips on the right half in th center, fanning them out. Place one piece of salmon on the fanned parsr Add half the garlic, half the lemon slices, half the thyme, ½ teaspoon of virgin olive oil, and a pinch each of kosher salt and pepper.

6. Seal the packet by folding the left half of the heart over the right side. Fc along the edge of the heart and create a seal. Repeat with the other piece parchment.

7. Place the packets on the empty side of the baking sheet and bake until tl salmon is cooked through, 10 to 15 minutes. Allow the fish to rest a few minutes before serving with the roasted green beans and remaining lem wedges.

8. Store any leftovers in an airtight container in the refrigerator for 1 to 2 c

VARIATION: There are many possibilities for spices and herbs to use with salmon. Favorites of mine include tarragon, thyme, and lemon. If I'm lucky enough to have lavender, I'll add some of that, too. Very French!

Per serving: Calories: 378; Total fat: 19g; Carbohydrates: 31g; Fiber: 9g; Protein: 26g; Calcium: 104mg; Vitamin D: 12mcg; Vitamin B$_{12}$: 0mcg; Iron: 3mg; Zinc: 1mg

Cherry Barbecue Chicken Cutlets

Serves 4 / Prep time: 10 minutes / Cook time: 5 minutes
5-INGREDIENT, GLUTEN-FREE

Chicken remains undefeated as the go-to dinner protein. Boneless, skinless chicken cutlets are the fastest to cook, but if you have more time, you can also use other cuts of chicken. Many supermarkets carry chicken cutlets, but you can also prepare your own. Carefully cut the chicken breasts horizontally in half and pound them to a quarter-inch thickness between sheets of plastic wrap to reduce any mess. Consider serving these with Avocado Slaw or Sautéed Lemon Broccoli and Kale on the side.

1½ pounds boneless, skinless chicken cutlets

1 recipe Cherry Barbecue Sauce or store-bought, divided

1½ tablespoons extra-virgin olive oil

STOVETOP METHOD

1. Marinate the chicken in half the barbecue sauce in the refrigerator for u day.

2. The following day, heat the extra-virgin olive oil in a large skillet over hi heat. Add the cutlets and cook without disturbing them. Make sure they not touch, about 1 to 2 inches apart. Cook until brown, 2 to 3 minutes. F and cook another 30 seconds.

3. Repeat with the remaining chicken cutlets if they do not all fit in one pa without overcrowding.

4. Allow the chicken to rest for 5 minutes before serving.

5. Meanwhile, heat the remaining sauce in a small saucepan, then serve wi cooked chicken.

GRILL METHOD

1. Marinate the chicken in half the barbecue sauce in the refrigerator for u day.

2. Remove the chicken from the marinade and place it on a plate, removin excess sauce. Discard the marinade.

3. Place the remaining sauce in a small saucepan over low heat until warm

4. Prepare the grill grates and heat them to between 425°F and 450°F.

5. When the grill is hot, lightly oil the cooking grate, arrange the cutlets ab inches apart, and cook for 2 to 3 minutes. Turn the cutlets over and grill cooked through, about 30 seconds more.

6. Let the grilled cutlets rest for 5 minutes before serving them with the remaining warm sauce. Store any leftovers in an airtight container in th refrigerator for 1 to 2 days.

MAKE IT EASIER: If you have a favorite barbecue sauce, go ahead and use it, but check the nutrition label. Most store-bought barbecue sauces are quite high in carbohydrates, sugar, and sodium.

Per serving: Calories: 272; Total fat: 6g; Carbohydrates: 16g; Fiber: 3g; Protein: 40g; Calcium: 36mg; Vitamin D: 0mcg; Vitamin B$_{12}$: 0mcg; Iron: 1mg; Zinc: <1mg

Miso Skirt Steak

Serves 4 / Prep time: 20 minutes / Cook time: 5 to 10 minutes

I promised you in the introduction that you would see a few favorites and, yes, that means this perfectly prepared steak. Red meat can fit into a healthy diet, as long as it's in moderation and your focus is still on whole, plant-based foods. While meat shouldn't be the primary source of your calories or macronutrients, know that you can still enjoy steak on occasion. Here it is, flavorfully prepared with miso and soy.

3 tablespoons yellow miso

1 tablespoon low-sodium soy sauce or tamari

1/2 tablespoon sesame oil

2 tablespoons chile-garlic sauce

1 1/2 pounds skirt steak, patted dry

3 tablespoons rice vinegar

1 tablespoon vegetable oil, divided

1. In a medium bowl, whisk together the miso, soy sauce, sesame oil, and c garlic sauce. Put 1 tablespoon of the sauce in a separate small bowl and s aside. Place the steak in the bowl with the remaining sauce and marinat room temperature for 10 to 15 minutes.

2. Stir the vinegar and 1/2 tablespoon of vegetable oil into the reserved sau set aside.

3. Remove the steak from the bowl and pat it dry.

4. Heat the remaining 1/2 tablespoon of vegetable oil in a large skillet over medium-high heat, add the steak, and cook without disturbing it. Cook to 3 minutes, until brown. Flip the steak and repeat with the other side (to 125°F internal temperature for medium rare and 135°F for medium). Transfer the steak to a plate, tent it with foil, and allow it to rest for 5 to minutes.

5. Serve with the sauce on the side.

NUTRIENT BOOST: Keep the meal simple and serve the steak with salad greens, cooked whole grains, Cauliflower Rice, or a mixture of all three options.

Per serving: Calories: 478; Total fat: 36g; Carbohydrates: 4g; Fiber: 1g; Protein: 32g; Calcium: 10mg; Vitamin D: 0mcg; Vitamin B$_{12}$: <1mcg; Iron: 3mg; Zinc: <1mg

Herbed Buttermilk Chicken

Serves 4 / Prep time: 5 minutes / Cook time: 25 minutes
GLUTEN-FREE, ONE PAN

The chicken in this exceptional dish needs to be marinated in the buttermilk seasoning (brine), so you will need to plan ahead when you make it, but it cooks quite quickly after that. Marinating will not only help tenderize your bird, but it will also give the poultry a deep, rich flavor. Try serving this with Herbed Tomato Salad to round out the meal.

1½ pounds boneless, skinless chicken breasts

4 cups buttermilk

Pinch kosher salt

Pinch freshly ground black pepper

1 cup thinly sliced yellow onion

2 tablespoons canola oil

¼ cup Italian seasoning

1 lemon, cut into wedges

1. In a large bowl or sealable plastic bag, combine the chicken, buttermilk, and pepper. Cover or seal and refrigerate for at least 1 hour and up to 24 hours.

2. When the chicken is ready to cook, preheat the oven to 425°F. Line a bal sheet with parchment paper.

3. Remove the chicken from the buttermilk brine and pat it dry. Place the chicken on the prepared baking sheet along with the onion, and drizzle everything with the canola oil. Toss together on the baking sheet (this w save you a bowl) to coat the chicken and onion evenly.

4. Bake for 25 minutes or until the chicken is cooked through. (If the chick thick, you can cut the breasts in half lengthwise. It will cut down on you time by half or less. Check the chicken after it's cooked for 8 minutes if t breasts are thin.)

5. Allow the chicken to rest and sprinkle it and the onions with the Italian seasoning.

6. Serve with a squeeze of lemon juice.

INGREDIENT TIP: If you don't have Italian seasoning at home, it can be substituted with a combination of thyme, oregano, parsley, basil, or marjoram. Use a blend of whichever you have on hand. You can also use the Middle Eastern spice blend za'atar with this recipe.

Per serving: Calories: 437; Total fat: 20g; Carbohydrates: 19g; Fiber: 2g; Protein: 46g; Calcium: 352mg; Vitamin D: 3mcg; Vitamin B_{12}: 1mcg; Iron: 3mg; Zinc: 1mg

Chicken Sausage and Cauliflower Pizza

Serves 2 to 4 / Prep time: 5 minutes / Cook time: 10 minutes
5-INGREDIENT, GLUTEN-FREE, ONE PAN

As little as five years ago, you would have had to make your own cauliflower pizza crust because this product was not on the culinary radar. Now even small grocery stores carry cauliflower pizza crust as a substitute for wheat-based crusts. If you prefer, you can use pita, naan, or sliced vegetables (eggplant or zucchini, for example) as the pizza base instead of the store-bought crust with delicious results.

1 store-bought cauliflower pizza crust, thawed

¼ cup Basic Marinara or store-bought

1 link cooked chicken sausage, casing removed, sliced

1 red bell pepper, diced

2 ounces shredded mozzarella cheese

1. Preheat the oven according to the cauliflower pizza crust's package instructions.

2. Place the cauliflower crust on a baking sheet and spread it evenly with tl marinara sauce. Evenly distribute the chicken sausage, bell pepper, and mozzarella cheese on the pizza.

3. Bake the pizza according to instructions, usually 7 to 10 minutes if bake 425°F.

4. Slice and serve.

5. Store any leftovers in an airtight container in the refrigerator for 3 to 4 (

VARIATION: The options for pizza toppings are endless. Add any vegetables—like small broccoli florets, cooked mushrooms, diced onions, olives, canned artichokes, fresh tomatoes, fresh herbs, or even salad greens—to the sauce-covered crust and bake.

Per serving: Calories: 408; Total fat: 16g; Carbohydrates: 49g; Fiber: 3g; Protein: 15g; Calcium: 203mg; Vitamin D: <1mcg; Vitamin B$_{12}$: <1mcg; Iron: 1mg; Zinc: 1mg

Turkey Bolognese with Chickpea Pasta

Serves 4 / Prep time: 5 minutes / Cook time: 25 minutes
GLUTEN-FREE, HIGH-FIBER

Making traditional Bolognese sauce is a long and arduous process. The classic Italian dish made with pork and beef can take all day. But I've come up with a recipe that is much faster and has fewer carbs. Chickpea pasta is a tasty alternative to wheat-based pasta with fewer carbohydrates and more protein and fiber, so it leaves your tummy fuller for longer. Preparing the vegetables for the sauce in a food processor cuts down on time considerably.

1 onion, coarsely chopped

1 large carrot, coarsely chopped

2 celery stalks, coarsely chopped

1 tablespoon extra-virgin olive oil

1 pound ground turkey

½ cup milk

¾ cup red or white wine

1 (28-ounce) can diced tomatoes

10 ounces cooked chickpea pasta

1. Place the onion, carrots, and celery in a food processor and pulse until fi chopped.

2. Heat the extra-virgin olive oil in a Dutch oven or medium skillet over medium-high heat. Sauté the chopped vegetables for 3 to 5 minutes, or softened. Add the ground turkey, breaking the poultry into smaller piec and cook for 5 minutes.

3. Add the milk and wine and cook until the liquid is nearly evaporated (tu the heat to high to quicken the process).

4. Add the tomatoes and bring the sauce to a simmer. Reduce the heat to lc and simmer for 10 to 15 minutes.

5. Meanwhile, cook the pasta according to the package instructions and se aside.

6. Serve the sauce with the cooked chickpea pasta.

7. Store any leftovers in an airtight container in the refrigerator for 3 to 4 (

Per serving: Calories: 601; Total fat: 23g; Carbohydrates: 58g; Fiber: 11g; Protein: 39g; Calcium: 146mg; Vitamin D: 1mcg; Vitamin B$_{12}$: 2mcg; Iron: 7mg; Zinc: 3mg

Green Bean and Radish Potato Salad

CHAPTER SEVEN
Sides and Snacks

Sides and snacks are often treated as an afterthought, not given the same consideration as large-plate main courses, or dessert. But 33 percent of Americans snack at least once per day (according to a 2019 survey from the International Food Information Council), and some statistics have that number as high as 94 percent (Mintel, 2015). Similarly, a supplementary side dish with your main course is also a common feature of dining. We tackle small plates in this chapter and take particular care because the "extras" like snacks and sides can be one of the most important factors when trying to cut back on carbs. You'll recognize some classics here, as well as variations on those classics. For example, kale chip nachos are a surprisingly satisfying alternative to the traditional corn tortilla chip dish. When trying to keep yourself satisfied throughout the day, this could be the most crucial section of the book.

e

Cucumber Roll-Ups

Eggplant Pizzas

Roasted Carrot and Chickpea Dip

Kale Chip Nachos

Lemony White Bean Puree

Green Bean and Radish Potato Salad

Sautéed Lemon Broccoli and Kale

Roasted Asparagus with Romesco Sauce

Charred Sesame Broccoli

Smashed Cucumber Salad

Garlic Roasted Radishes

Cauliflower Rice

Cajun-Style Collards

Mashed Sweet Potatoes

Charred Miso Cabbage

Avocado Slaw

Cucumber Roll-Ups

Serves 2 to 4 / Prep time: 5 minutes

5-INGREDIENT, GLUTEN-FREE, NO-COOK, ONE BOWL, VEGETARIAN

Roll-ups are easy to make and ideal for a grab-and-go snack. Use any wrap you'd like for this recipe and read your labels to ensure the carbs are within your personal limit. Some of my favorite wraps are the raw vegetable versions (cauliflower, kale, tomato) or those with a base of almond flour, coconut, corn, whole wheat (lavash), or potato lefse.

2 (6-inch) gluten-free wraps

2 tablespoons cream cheese

1 medium cucumber, cut into long strips

2 tablespoons fresh mint

1. Place the wraps on your work surface and spread them evenly with the cheese. Top with the cucumber and mint.

2. Roll the wraps up from one side to the other, kind of like a burrito. Slice 1-inch bites or keep whole.

3. Serve.

4. Store any leftovers in an airtight container in the refrigerator for 1 to 2 (

MAKE IT EASIER: Depending on the flexibility of the wrap you've chosen, rolling this snack can be challenging. If the product is stiff, try microwaving it for a few seconds to soften it or warming it in a dry skillet over low heat.

Per serving: Calories: 168; Total fat: 8g; Carbohydrates: 21g; Fiber: 3g; Protein: 5g; Calcium: 35mg; Vitamin D: 0mcg; Vitamin B$_{12}$: <1mcg; Iron: <1mg; Zinc: <1mg

Eggplant Pizzas

Serves 4 to 6 / Prep time: 5 minutes / Cook time: 15 minutes
GLUTEN-FREE, HIGH-FIBER, VEGETARIAN

There was a story once of a young boy who simply *hated* eggplant, and couldn't stand the sight of this vegetable. What did his mother do to ensure he was getting the fiber, potassium, and the B vitamins found in this nightshade? Turn it into pizza, of course. You're sure to enjoy this light pizza and extra serving of vegetables, too.

2 pounds eggplant, cut into ½-inch-thick slices

2 tablespoons extra-virgin olive oil

Kosher salt

Freshly ground black pepper

1 cup Basic Marinara or store-bought

1 cup crushed tomatoes

½ onion, thinly sliced

1 cup sliced mushrooms

1½ cups shredded mozzarella cheese

1. Preheat the oven to 425°F. Line a baking sheet with parchment paper.

2. Brush both sides of the eggplant slices with extra-virgin olive oil and ligh season them with salt and pepper. Place the slices on the prepared bakir sheet and bake until the top side of the eggplant browns, about 7 minute

3. Meanwhile, in a small bowl, stir together the marinara and crushed tom until combined.

4. When the eggplant is browned, turn the slices over. Top them with mari followed by the onions and mushrooms. Sprinkle with the cheese and b; until the cheese melts, 5 to 8 minutes.

5. Serve immediately.

6. Store any leftovers in an airtight container in the refrigerator for 3 to 4 (

MAKE IT EASIER: You can also use a toaster oven to make this tempting snack. It will heat the pizzas much faster and easier if you have one on hand.

Per serving: Calories: 268; Total fat: 15g; Carbohydrates: 24g; Fiber: 9g; Protein: 12g; Calcium: 257mg; Vitamin D: <1mcg; Vitamin B$_{12}$: <1mcg; Iron: 1mg; Zinc: 2mg

Roasted Carrot and Chickpea Dip

Makes 3 cups / Prep time: 10 minutes / Cook time: 15 minutes
GLUTEN-FREE, VEGETARIAN

Dips are often crowd favorites at parties because you don't just get to sample the dip itself, you also enjoy an assortment of "dippers." It is like having two snacks in one! This sweet and spicy dip is ideal for a group, but it is just as good when you're looking for your own snack. It keeps well, so make it in advance to have on hand when you're feeling hungry.

4 medium carrots, quartered lengthwise

¼ cup plus 2 teaspoons extra-virgin olive oil, divided

Pinch kosher salt

Pinch freshly ground black pepper

1 (15-ounce) can chickpeas, drained and rinsed

1 garlic clove, minced

1 red chile (optional)

Zest and juice of 1 lemon

2 tablespoons tahini

1 tablespoon Harissa

½ teaspoon ground cumin

¼ teaspoon ground coriander

Pomegranate arils (seeds) (optional)

Cilantro, chopped (optional)

1. Preheat the oven to 425°F. Line a baking sheet with parchment paper.

2. In a medium bowl, toss the carrots with 2 teaspoons of extra-virgin oliv the salt, and the pepper. Spread them in a single layer on the prepared b sheet and roast until tender, about 15 minutes. Turn the carrots over ha through.

3. Meanwhile, place the chickpeas, garlic, chile, lemon zest and juice, tahir harissa, cumin, and coriander in a food processor. Set aside. Add the car to the processor when they are cooked. Pulse until the mixture is coarse Scrape the bowl down, then turn the processor back on while you drizzl remaining ¼ cup of extra-virgin olive oil through the feed tube of the machine. Adjust the seasonings as desired. If it's too thick, add water to

4. Top with pomegranate seeds and chopped cilantro (if using,) and Serve cut vegetables.

5. Store any leftovers in an airtight container in the refrigerator for up to 4

SUBSTITUTION TIP: Use tomato paste instead of harissa if you don't have it ready, or if you want less spice.

Per ¼-cup serving: Calories: 105; Total fat: 7g; Carbohydrates: 8g; Fiber: 2g; Protein: 2g; Calcium: 29mg; Vitamin D: 0mcg; Vitamin B_{12}: 0mcg; Iron: 1mg; Zinc: <1mg

Kale Chip Nachos

Serves 2 to 4 / Prep time: 10 minutes / Cook time: 20 minutes
GLUTEN-FREE, HIGH-FIBER, VEGETARIAN

Kale was everywhere for a while, a "superfood" that seemed to descend into a parody considering its appearance in so many different products and recipes. But, as it turns out, there was something to the hype after all. And when you're looking for something to snack on while watching the game or your favorite show, you want to make sure it's something that isn't going to do too much damage to your body in the long run. This version of nachos uses kale as the base, so you can snack away while getting the nutritional boost that comes from this hearty green alongside sweet potato and black beans.

1 bunch kale, torn into bite-size pieces

3 tablespoons extra-virgin olive oil, divided

2 teaspoons ground cumin, divided

1 large sweet potato, cut into ¼-inch-thick rounds

1 (15-ounce) can black beans, rinsed and drained

½ teaspoon ground coriander

1 teaspoon chili powder

OPTIONAL TOPPINGS
Avocado slices

Salsa

Jicama, sliced

Red onion, sliced

Fresh cilantro

Fresh chiles, minced

Fresh tomatoes, diced

1. Preheat the oven to 225°F. Line a baking sheet with parchment paper.

2. In a large bowl, toss the kale with 1 tablespoon of oil and 1 teaspoon of cι
   Use your hands to massage the kale and evenly distribute the oil.

3. Spread the kale in a single even layer on the prepared baking sheet. (Yoι
   need two lined baking sheets for this.) Bake for 15 minutes, then flip anc
   and bake for another 5 to 10 minutes.

4. Meanwhile, heat 1 tablespoon of oil in a large skillet over medium-high l
   Arrange the sweet potato rounds in a single layer in the skillet, cover, an
   them cook until they begin to brown on the bottom, about 3 minutes. Fl
   potatoes over and cook for 3 to 5 minutes more.

5. Add the black beans to the skillet with the remaining 1 tablespoon of oil
   remaining 1 teaspoon of cumin, the coriander, and chili powder. Cook fc
   minutes, then set aside and keep warm if the kale is not yet finished bak

6. Serve on a platter, starting with the kale as a base, topped with sweet
   potatoes, black beans, and finally, any optional toppings.

7. Store any leftovers in an airtight container in the refrigerator for 3 to 4 ι

VARIATION: You can use any kind of canned beans or lentils in place of the black beans
for additional variety with this recipe.

Per serving: Calories: 504; Total fat: 23g; Carbohydrates: 63g; Fiber: 21g; Protein:
16g; Calcium: 266mg; Vitamin D: 0mcg; Vitamin B_{12}: 0mcg; Iron: 7mg; Zinc: 2mg

Lemony White Bean Puree

Makes ~2 cups / Prep time: 10 minutes
GLUTEN-FREE, HIGH-FIBER, NO-COOK, VEGETARIAN

This recipe calls for herbs de Provence, an essential herb blend native to the southern region of France. You may see it appear in other Mediterranean cuisines. It adds a distinct flavor to dishes like chicken, roasted vegetables, and grilled fish. There are many variations of the herb blend, but you will usually find basil, fennel, marjoram, parsley, rosemary, tarragon, and thyme. Some blends include lavender as well.

1 (15-ounce) can white beans, drained and rinsed

1 small onion, coarsely chopped

1 garlic clove, minced

Zest and juice of 1 lemon

½ teaspoon herbs de Provence

3 tablespoons extra-virgin olive oil, divided

1 tablespoon chopped fresh parsley

1. Place the beans, onion, garlic, lemon zest and juice, and herbs in a food processor and pulse until smooth. While the machine is running, slowly stream in 2 tablespoons of extra-virgin olive oil. If the mixture is too thi add water very slowly until you've reached the desired consistency.

2. Transfer the puree to a medium serving bowl. Top with the remaining 1 tablespoon of extra-virgin olive oil and the parsley.

3. Serve with your favorite vegetable or flatbread of choice. Store any lefto in an airtight container in the refrigerator for up to 4 days.

VARIATION: Other dried herbs can be substituted for herbs de Provence. Choose one or more of the dried herbs listed here and alter the dip to your liking.

Per ½-cup serving: Calories: 197; Total fat: 11g; Carbohydrates: 21g; Fiber: 6g; Protein: 6g; Calcium: 78mg; Vitamin D: 0mcg; Vitamin B$_{12}$: 0mcg; Iron: 2mg; Zinc:

<1mg

Green Bean and Radish Potato Salad

Serves 6 / Prep time: 10 minutes / Cook time: 20 minutes
GLUTEN-FREE, ONE POT, VEGETARIAN

Fingerling potatoes, those small multicolored potatoes similar in size to fingers (hence their name), have a robust, earthy, and buttery flavor. They are wonderful in salads because they keep their shape after cooking due to their firmness. If you cannot find fingerlings, Yukon Gold potatoes will also work in this recipe.

Kosher salt

6 ounces fresh green beans, trimmed and cut into 1-inch pieces

1½ pounds fingerling potatoes

⅓ cup extra-virgin olive oil

2 tablespoons freshly squeezed lemon juice

1 tablespoon Dijon or whole-grain mustard

1 shallot, minced

8 radishes, thinly sliced

¼ cup fresh dill, chopped

Freshly ground black pepper

1. Place a small saucepan filled three-quarters full of water and a pinch of s over high heat and bring it to a boil. Add the green beans and boil for 2 minutes, then transfer them with a slotted spoon to a colander. Run the under cold running water until cool and transfer to a medium bowl.

2. Place the potatoes in the same pot of boiling water, reduce the heat to lo and simmer until tender, about 12 minutes.

3. Meanwhile, combine the extra-virgin olive oil, lemon juice, mustard, an shallot in a jar. Seal with the lid and shake vigorously. If you don't have a with a fitted lid, you can also whisk the ingredients in a bowl.

4. Transfer the cooked potatoes to a colander and cool them under cold ru water. When they're cool enough to handle, slice the potatoes into thin

rounds.

5. Add the potatoes and dressing to the bowl with the green beans, along w
   the radishes and dill, and toss to combine.

6. Season with salt and pepper and serve.

7. Store any leftovers in an airtight container in the refrigerator for 3 to 4

Per serving: Calories: 208; Total fat: 12g; Carbohydrates: 24g; Fiber: 3g; Protein:
3g; Calcium: 33mg; Vitamin D: 0mcg; Vitamin B$_{12}$: 0mcg; Iron: 3mg; Zinc: <1mg

Sautéed Lemon Broccoli and Kale

Serves 4 to 6 / Prep time: 5 minutes / Cook time: 15 minutes
GLUTEN-FREE, HIGH-FIBER, VEGETARIAN

This dish celebrates green vegetables—something parents have struggled to get their children to eat for decades. It is simple dishes like this one that remind us that green vegetables can be just as flavorful as anything that comes from an animal. Cumin seeds, which make everything better, garlic, and a punch of flavor from fresh lemon should convince even the most skeptical of diners to eat their greens.

1 large head broccoli, cut into small florets

2 tablespoons extra-virgin olive oil

1 bunch kale, torn into 1- to 2-inch pieces

2 garlic cloves, minced

½ teaspoon cumin seeds

1 lemon, cut into wedges

1. Bring a medium saucepan filled three-quarters full of water to a boil ove heat. Add the broccoli and boil for 3 minutes. Drain the broccoli and rur under cold water until completely cool.

2. Heat the extra-virgin olive oil in a large skillet over medium-high heat. / the broccoli, kale, garlic, and cumin and sauté for 2 to 3 minutes. Remov skillet from the heat and serve with freshly squeezed lemon.

3. Store any leftovers in an airtight container in the refrigerator for 3 to 4 (

VARIATION: Add other citrus or herbs to boost the flavor profile of the dish. Toss in red pepper flakes while you're at it for a touch of heat. This side pairs beautifully with any protein-heavy entrée like <u>Miso Skirt Steak</u>.

Per serving: Calories: 126; Total fat: 8g; Carbohydrates: 13g; Fiber: 5g; Protein: 5g; Calcium: 134mg; Vitamin D: 0mcg; Vitamin B$_{12}$: 0mcg; Iron: 2mg; Zinc: 1mg

Roasted Asparagus with Romesco Sauce

Serves 2 to 4 / Prep time: 5 minutes / Cook time: 15 minutes
5-INGREDIENT, HIGH-FIBER, VEGETARIAN

Asparagus is one of the true harbingers of warm weather, along with the birdsongs and delicate budding flowers, of course. The moment fresh asparagus becomes available, try this lovely side dish to celebrate the season. The Romesco Sauce brings out the natural, earthy flavor of the asparagus and adds a punch of its own to create a perfect balance. You can roast or grill the asparagus—both are equally tasty.

1 bunch asparagus, woody ends removed

1 tablespoon extra-virgin olive oil

¼ to ½ cup Romesco Sauce or store-bought

ROASTED METHOD

1. Preheat the oven to 425°F. Line a baking sheet with parchment paper.

2. In a medium bowl, toss the asparagus with the extra-virgin olive oil.

3. Place the asparagus on the baking sheet and roast until tender, 12 to 15 minutes.

4. Remove the asparagus from the heat, arrange it on a serving platter, top with romesco sauce, and serve.

GRILL METHOD

1. Preheat the grill to high heat.

2. In a medium bowl, toss the asparagus with the extra-virgin olive oil.

3. Place the asparagus on a grill pan or directly on the grill grates and sear to 4 minutes until tender, turning them as often as you need to avoid bu

4. Remove the asparagus from the heat, arrange it on a serving platter, top with romesco sauce, and serve.

5. Store any leftovers in an airtight container in the refrigerator for 3 to 4 (

VARIATION: Instead of Romesco Sauce, accent the asparagus with citrus by tossing the spears in <u>Lemon Vinaigrette Dressing</u>. No need to use additional oil, just the asparagus and the dressing work fine.

Per serving: Calories: 183; Total fat: 13g; Carbohydrates: 14g; Fiber: 6g; Protein: 7g; Calcium: 80mg; Vitamin D: 0mcg; Vitamin B$_{12}$: 0mcg; Iron: 5mg; Zinc: 2mg

Charred Sesame Broccoli

Serves 4 / Prep time: 5 minutes / Cook time: 15 minutes
5-INGREDIENT, VEGETARIAN

Broccoli is ubiquitous, but often people use the same techniques and overcook until it's army green in color and turns to mush. This is highly undesirable in both appearance and flavor. Try cooking your broccoli using this method and you'll have everyone reaching for it. Broccoli is loaded with fiber, calcium, folate, potassium, and iron and supports bone health, brain function, and heart health.

1 tablespoon extra-virgin olive oil

1 tablespoon low-sodium soy sauce

½ tablespoon sesame oil

1 head broccoli

1 tablespoon toasted sesame seeds

1. Preheat the oven to 450°F. Line a baking sheet with parchment paper.

2. In a medium bowl, whisk together the extra-virgin olive oil, soy sauce, a sesame oil. Add the broccoli and toss to evenly coat it.

3. Spread the coated broccoli on the prepared baking sheet and bake for 1C minutes, until tender.

4. Remove the sheet from the oven, flip the broccoli over, and return it to t oven for an additional 5 to 10 minutes.

5. Serve the broccoli with toasted sesame seeds on top.

6. Store any leftovers in an airtight container in the refrigerator for up to 4

INGREDIENT TIP: You can use regular broccoli here, but also give Chinese broccoli a try if it's available. Called *gai lan,* it is one of the most popular greens in all of China and has a stronger, slightly bitter note that lends itself well to the sesame and the soy of this dish. Broccoli rabe is also an inspired choice.

Per serving: Calories: 110; Total fat: 7g; Carbohydrates: 11g; Fiber: 4g; Protein: 5g; Calcium: 75mg; Vitamin D: 0mcg; Vitamin B$_{12}$: 0mcg; Iron: 1mg; Zinc: 1mg

Smashed Cucumber Salad

Serves 4 to 6 / Prep time: 10 minutes
GLUTEN-FREE, NO-COOK, VEGETARIAN

Smashing cucumbers for a salad is a standard technique in many parts of Asia. Once you've tried it, you'll understand why it's such a great idea, and not just for taking out your aggression. Smashing a cucumber changes the way it picks up the flavors. More cucumber cells open up and allow for some water to escape, while absorbing other added ingredients, thus changing the overall taste.

2 pounds mini cucumbers (English or Persian), unpeeled

½ teaspoon kosher salt

1 tablespoon extra-virgin olive oil

¾ teaspoon ground cumin

¼ teaspoon turmeric

Juice of 1 lime

½ cup cilantro leaves

1. Cut the cucumbers crosswise into 4-inch pieces and again in half length

2. On a work surface, place one cucumber, flesh-side down. Place the side knife blade on the cucumber and carefully smash down lightly with you hand. Alternatively, put in a plastic bag, seal, and smash with a rolling pi similar tool. Be careful not to break the bag. The skin of the cucumber sl crack and flesh will break away. Repeat with all the cucumbers and cut t smashed pieces on a bias into bite-size pieces.

3. Transfer the cucumber pieces to a strainer and toss them with the salt. the cucumbers to rest for at least 15 minutes.

4. Meanwhile, prepare the dressing by whisking together the extra-virgin oil, cumin, turmeric, and lime juice in a small bowl.

5. When the cucumbers are ready, shake them to remove any excess liquid Transfer the cucumbers to a large bowl with the dressing and cilantro a

toss to combine. Serve.

6. Store any leftovers in an airtight container in the refrigerator for up to 2

MAKE IT EASIER: Use fresh, firm-fleshed cucumbers and avoid those that are older and soft. Your standard greenhouse variety commonly found in grocery stores will work just fine, but I would strongly suggest removing the seeds before smashing them.

Per serving: Calories: 69; Total fat: 4g; Carbohydrates: 10g; Fiber: 3g; Protein: 2g; Calcium: 44mg; Vitamin D: 0mcg; Vitamin B_{12}: 0mcg; Iron: 1mg; Zinc: 1mg

Garlic Roasted Radishes

Serves 2 to 4 / Prep time: 5 minutes / Cook time: 15 minutes
5-INGREDIENT, GLUTEN-FREE, VEGETARIAN

Radishes are one of spring's greatest treats. They are cruciferous, like broccoli and cabbage, which means they have many of the same cancer-fighting compounds as these powerhouse vegetables. They also have a positive impact on the fight against diabetes, as some studies suggest eating radishes may help improve blood sugar control. Radishes are also delicious and come in a multitude of colors that look great on the plate.

1 pound radishes, halved

1 tablespoon canola oil

Pinch kosher salt

4 garlic cloves, thinly sliced

¼ cup chopped fresh dill

1. Preheat the oven to 425°F. Line a baking sheet with parchment paper.

2. In a medium bowl, toss the radishes with the canola oil and salt. Spread vegetables on the prepared baking sheet and roast for 10 minutes. Remo the sheet from the oven, add the garlic, mix well, and return to the oven minutes.

3. Remove the radishes from the oven, adjust the seasoning as desired, and serve topped with dill on a serving plate or as a side dish.

4. Store any leftovers in an airtight container in the refrigerator for 3 to 4

VARIATION: This salad can be exceptionally pretty if you use a variety of radishes. Look for watermelon radish, Easter egg, purple ninja, cherriette, or daikon if you want to experiment with colors. If you decide to take this route, cut the radishes to a similar size before roasting, so they cook at the same rate.

Per serving: Calories: 105; Total fat: 7g; Carbohydrates: 10g; Fiber: 4g; Protein: 2g; Calcium: 70mg; Vitamin D: 0mcg; Vitamin B_{12}: 0mcg; Iron: 1mg; Zinc: 1mg

Cauliflower Rice

Makes 2½ cups / Prep time: 5 minutes / Cook time: 5 minutes
5-INGREDIENT, GLUTEN-FREE, VEGETARIAN

Cauliflower rice cooks much faster than regular rice, so it can cut down on the cooking time if you use it in dishes like the Cauli-Lettuce Wraps or Tuna Poke with Riced Broccoli. This side dish is also a wonderful replacement for grains in general, especially when you have other carbohydrates in your meal that could cross over into excessive amounts.

1½ pounds cauliflower, coarsely chopped

½ tablespoon extra-virgin olive oil

Kosher salt

Freshly ground black pepper

1. Pulse the cauliflower in a food processor until it has a crumbly texture, almost like rice. Be careful not to over-pulse and make it too fine. It's ok have some larger chunks. Another option is to use a box grater if you do have a food processor. Put the crumbled cauliflower in a bowl and set as

2. Heat the oil in a large skillet over medium-high heat. Add the cauliflowe it with hot oil, and sauté 3 to 5 minutes. Season with salt and pepper anc serve.

3. Store any leftovers in an airtight container in the refrigerator for 3 to 4

VARIATION: Add any spice blend you want to jazz up the flavor of this rice. Try curry powder or add some fresh cilantro with lime, or fresh parsley with lemon.

Per ½-cup serving: Calories: 46; Total fat: 2g; Carbohydrates: 7g; Fiber: 3g; Protein: 3g; Calcium: 30mg; Vitamin D: 0mcg; Vitamin B$_{12}$: 0mcg; Iron: 1mg; Zinc: <1mg

Cajun-Style Collards

Serves 4 to 6 / Prep time: 10 minutes / Cook time: 20 minutes
GLUTEN-FREE, HIGH-FIBER, ONE POT, VEGETARIAN

This recipe pays tribute to the wonderful cuisine of Louisiana and helps illustrate the diversity of bountiful Southern lands. Southern cooking has a bad reputation for being a heavier or unhealthy cuisine because traditionally long workdays and tough schedules once called for calorie-dense meals. This style of cooking draws inspiration from all across the world and deserves its place in the pantheon of American dining.

2 tablespoons extra-virgin olive oil

½ large onion, chopped

1 pound collard greens, chopped

1 garlic clove, minced

½ teaspoon cayenne

3 cups low-sodium vegetable broth

2 tomatoes, diced

1. Heat the extra-virgin olive oil in a large stockpot over medium heat. Sau onion until slightly softened and translucent, about 2 minutes.

2. Add the collards, garlic, and cayenne and cook for 2 to 3 minutes. Add th vegetable broth, cover, and bring the mixture to a simmer.

3. Simmer until the greens are tender, about 15 minutes. Add the tomatoe adjust the seasonings as desired, and serve.

4. Store any leftovers in an airtight container in the refrigerator for 3 to 4

MAKE IT EASIER: This dish also tastes great with canned tomatoes instead of fresh. If substituting, add one cup along with the vegetable broth.

Per serving: Calories: 127; Total fat: 8g; Carbohydrates: 13g; Fiber: 6g; Protein: 4g; Calcium: 290mg; Vitamin D: 0mcg; Vitamin B_{12}: 0mcg; Iron: 1mg; Zinc: <1mg

Mashed Sweet Potatoes

Serves 6 to 8 / Prep time: 10 minutes / Cook time: 20 minutes
GLUTEN-FREE, VEGETARIAN

Personally, I love the peels in my mashed potatoes, but you may prefer to omit them. There's more fiber in the peel, so try cooking the potatoes with the skins first to get that extra nutrition in. And yes, there's butter in this recipe. I'm sorry, but it's not mashed potatoes without *some* butter. As long as you are pairing this side dish with foods that are low in saturated fat (lean meats and plants), then butter can be part of a balanced diet.

2 medium sweet potatoes, cut into 1- to 2-inch cubes

4 medium carrots, cut into 1-inch cubes

6 garlic cloves, halved

¼ teaspoon kosher salt

2 tablespoons unsalted butter

⅓ cup unsweetened almond milk

Freshly ground black pepper

1. Place the potatoes, carrots, garlic, and salt in a large stockpot and cover with water by 1½ inches. Bring to a boil over high heat, reduce the heat medium-high, and simmer for 10 to 15 minutes, until the vegetables bec tender.

2. Drain the vegetables and return them to the pot. Add the butter and alm milk and mash until smooth with a potato masher. Season with pepper. out with water or more milk to reach the desired consistency. Serve.

3. Store any leftovers in an airtight container in the refrigerator for up to 4

VARIATION: Need more variety for your taste buds? Here are some of my favorite sweet potato mash-ups—be sure to try them all.

Miso + ginger

Molasses + sesame seeds

Ginger + lime

Curry + coconut

Per serving: Calories: 94; Total fat: 4g; Carbohydrates: 14g; Fiber: 3g; Protein: 1g; Calcium: 57mg; Vitamin D: <1mcg; Vitamin B$_{12}$: <1mcg; Iron: 1mg; Zinc: <1mg

Charred Miso Cabbage

Serves 4 / Prep time: 5 minutes / Cook time: 20 minutes
5-INGREDIENT, GLUTEN-FREE, HIGH-FIBER, VEGETARIAN

This is one of my absolute favorite small plates to make for myself and to share. The combination of flavors and the added punch that comes from charring is a culinary journey you will want to take again and again. The meaty, crunchy nature of the cabbage adapts very well to grilling; you might never make this vegetable any other way.

3 tablespoons avocado oil

1 head green cabbage, cut into 8 wedges

3 tablespoons yellow or white miso

2 tablespoons rice wine vinegar

1 lime, cut into 8 wedges

1. Preheat the oven to 400°F. Line a baking sheet with parchment paper.

2. Heat the avocado oil in a large cast-iron pan or skillet over high heat. Ar 2 or 3 cabbage wedges in the skillet and cook for about 3 minutes on eac until charred or lightly blackened. When they're seared on both sides, p the wedges on the baking sheet.

3. Repeat with the remaining wedges.

4. In a small bowl, mix the miso with the rice wine vinegar and brush it on cabbage wedges evenly. Bake the wedges for 10 minutes.

5. When the wedges come out of the oven, squeeze the lime juice on them. Serve.

6. Store any leftovers in an airtight container in the refrigerator for 2 to 3

SUBSTITUTION TIP: You've probably figured it out by now—that I'd tell you any vinegar will work just fine for this recipe. My first choice would be white wine, then cider, before distilled white vinegar. Use another plant-based oil in place of avocado if you prefer as well.

Per serving: Calories: 178; Total fat: 11g; Carbohydrates: 18g; Fiber: 6g; Protein: 5g; Calcium: 104mg; Vitamin D: 0mcg; Vitamin B$_{12}$: <1mcg; Iron: 2mg; Zinc: 1mg

Avocado Slaw

Serves 4 to 6 / Prep time: 15 minutes
GLUTEN-FREE, HIGH-FIBER, NO-COOK, VEGETARIAN

Avocado is a nutrient-dense food that is full of heart-healthy fat, and it belongs on more than just toast. It's also incredibly creamy and makes an ideal substitute for mayonnaise and other common ingredients found in dressings. This is a very versatile recipe. It can be enjoyed on its own as a salad or side or added to the Jackfruit Tacos, the Game-Day Burger, or the Turkey Pastrami and Pimento Cheese Sandwich.

1 avocado

⅓ cup water

3 tablespoons apple cider vinegar

1 tablespoon Dijon mustard

4 cups packed shredded cabbage (red, green, or mixed)

2 cups shredded carrot

Kosher salt

Freshly ground black pepper

1. Place the avocado, water, vinegar, and mustard in a blender and puree u smooth. Add water if needed until you've reached a thin consistency, m: the dressing easy to toss with the shredded vegetables.

2. In a large bowl, toss the cabbage and carrot with the dressing. Season to with salt and pepper and serve.

3. Store any leftovers in an airtight container in the refrigerator for up to ̃

VARIATION: Add other veggies to the slaw, like kale or jicama, to mix it up.

Per serving: Calories: 101; Total fat: 6g; Carbohydrates: 13g; Fiber: 6g; Protein: 2g; Calcium: 53mg; Vitamin D: 0mcg; Vitamin B_{12}: 0mcg; Iron: 1mg; Zinc: 1mg

Banana N'Ice Cream with Cocoa Nuts

CHAPTER EIGHT
Dessert

Finally, the chapter you've been waiting for since the beginning of the book! You've probably heard that sugar and sweets are your enemies. But the chief philosophy of this book remains that everything can be enjoyed *in moderation*. This applies to sweets, too. There is no reason to cut your favorite things out of your diet entirely, nor is it necessary to deny yourself the things that bring you joy. What I mean to say is, you don't have to sacrifice dessert to live a healthy life.

In this chapter, I introduce recipes that will satisfy any sweet tooth without sugar overload or too many saturated fats. Dessert is the most important component of a meal for some people, a joyous treat deserving of celebration. This chapter has everything you need to enjoy dessert in its entirety while still maintaining a balanced diet.

M

Watermelon-Lime Granita

Banana N'Ice Cream with Cocoa Nuts

Blueberry Chocolate Clusters

Superfood Brownie Bites

Poached Pears

Orange Praline with Yogurt

Coconut Macaroons

Chocolate Tahini Bombs

Watermelon-Lime Granita

Serves 10 / Prep time: 15 minutes / Freeze time: 2½ hours

5-INGREDIENT, GLUTEN-FREE, NO-COOK, VEGETARIAN

Cool and refreshing, this granita is perfect for the hot days of summer. While this recipe is quick and easy to make, it does require a bit of preplanning for it to taste best. The pureed fruit takes about 2½ hours to freeze and turn into a delicious slush, so make sure you plan ahead if serving this dessert.

1 pound seedless watermelon flesh, cut into 1-inch chunks

2 tablespoons agave syrup

2 tablespoons freshly squeezed lime juice

1. Line a baking sheet with parchment paper. Spread the watermelon chur a single layer on the sheet and freeze for at least 20 minutes.

2. Once the chunks are frozen, transfer them to a blender with the agave s and lime juice. Blend until liquefied and pour the mixture into a 9-by-13 shallow baking dish. Return to the freezer and freeze for 2 hours.

3. Every 30 minutes or so, take a fork and scrape the crystals into a slush consistency. Keep in the freezer for up to 1 month.

VARIATION: Surprise your palate and guests by adding a pinch of cayenne or chili powder to make the granita spicy. Substitute another type of citrus for the lime and different kinds of melon to create refreshing variations.

Per serving: Calories: 27; Total fat: <1g; Carbohydrates: 7g; Fiber: <1g; Protein: <1g; Calcium: 4mg; Vitamin D: 0mcg; Vitamin B$_{12}$: 0mcg; Iron: <1mg; Zinc: <1mg

Banana N'Ice Cream with Cocoa Nuts

Serves 4 to 6 / Prep time: 10 minutes / Cook time: 12 minutes
GLUTEN-FREE, HIGH-FIBER, VEGETARIAN

It seems like everyone has frozen bananas on hand, and boy do they pile up quickly. If you are in danger of a frozen banana avalanche every time you open the freezer, this is the recipe for you. If your frozen bananas are whole, you will have to give them a rough chop before adding them to the food processor. If you don't have any frozen bananas, slice fresh bananas into small pieces, freeze them for 3 hours or overnight, then follow the recipe.

FOR THE COCOA NUTS

¼ cup freshly squeezed orange juice

1 tablespoon coconut oil

2 teaspoons cocoa powder

½ teaspoon kosher salt

¼ teaspoon ground cinnamon

¼ teaspoon ground cardamom

½ teaspoon orange zest

1 cup raw almonds

FOR THE BANANA N'ICE CREAM

2 frozen, diced bananas

TO MAKE THE COCOA NUTS

1. Preheat the oven to 350°F. Line a baking sheet with parchment paper.

2. In a small saucepan, bring the orange juice to a boil over medium-high h reduce the heat to low, and simmer until the juice is reduced to about 2 tablespoons, 5 to 7 minutes. Add the coconut oil, stir until well combine remove from the heat. Whisk in the cocoa powder, salt, cinnamon, cardamom, and zest. Then add the almonds and stir to coat them. Sprea mixture onto the prepared baking sheet.

3. Bake the nuts for 10 to 12 minutes, stirring halfway through, until toaste
   Allow to cool.

4. Store the nuts in an airtight container at room temperature for up to 2 v

TO MAKE THE BANANA N'ICE CREAM

5. Put the frozen bananas in a food processor and pulse. Scrape down the s
   then pulse once more. Continue to do this for several minutes until the
   texture resembles ice cream. Serve immediately with the cooled nuts.

MAKE IT EASIER: Skip the nuts and only make the banana n'ice cream; that way, you only need one ingredient for a delectable dessert!

Per serving: Calories: 333; Total fat: 24g; Carbohydrates: 23g; Fiber: 6g; Protein: 8g; Calcium: 122mg; Vitamin D: 0mcg; Vitamin B_{12}: 0mcg; Iron: 2mg; Zinc: <1mg

Blueberry Chocolate Clusters

Serves 10 / Prep time: 5 minutes / Cook time: 5 minutes
5-INGREDIENT, GLUTEN-FREE, VEGETARIAN

We all grew up with Hershey's Kisses, and anyone who's ever been in a store around Valentine's Day has seen them in abundance. Making your own version is incredibly easy, and you don't have to wait for a holiday to enjoy them. Chocolate and blueberries are full of antioxidants and can help boost brain health.

1½ cups dark chocolate chips

1 tablespoon coconut oil, melted

½ cups chopped, toasted pecans

2 cups blueberries

1. Line a baking sheet with parchment paper.

2. Melt the chocolate in a microwave-safe bowl in 20- to 30-second interv:

3. In a medium bowl, combine the melted chocolate with the coconut oil a pecans.

4. Spoon a small amount of chocolate mixture (about 1 teaspoon) on the prepared baking sheet.

5. Place a cluster of about 5 blueberries on top of the chocolate. You shoul about 20 clusters in total.

6. Drizzle a small amount of chocolate over the berries.

7. Freeze until set, about 15 minutes.

8. Store in an airtight container in the refrigerator for up to 5 days or in th freezer for up to 1 month.

VARIATION: Any and all berries will do in these pretty clusters, and if you have any available, use a variety such as golden berry, raspberry, or mulberry. You could ditch the berries altogether and add other fresh fruit. Just be sure to cut the fruit into ¼-inch to ½-inch pieces.

Per serving: Calories: 230; Total fat: 17g; Carbohydrates: 18g; Fiber: 4g; Protein: 3g; Calcium: 26mg; Vitamin D: 0mcg; Vitamin B$_{12}$: <1mcg; Iron: 4mg; Zinc: 1mg

Superfood Brownie Bites

Makes 30 / Prep time: 15 minutes
GLUTEN-FREE, NO-COOK, VEGETARIAN

Words like "superfood" get tossed around often and, in most cases, without justification. What exactly qualifies an ingredient as a superfood? In this case, it's the combination of nuts, seeds, cacao, and naturally sweet dates, all of which offer benefits to your body. Show up to any party with a platter of these brownie bites and watch them disappear.

1 cup raw nuts (walnuts, pecans, or cashews)

½ cup hulled hemp seeds

⅓ cup raw pepitas

½ cup raw cacao powder

1 cup pitted dates

2 tablespoons coconut oil

1 teaspoon vanilla extract

1. Line a baking sheet with parchment paper.

2. Place the nuts, hemp seeds, and pepitas in a food processor and pulse ur the ingredients are a meal consistency. Add the cacao powder, dates, co oil, and vanilla extract and pulse until the mixture holds together if you it with your fingers. The dough should ball up and appear glossy, and no too sticky and wet. If it doesn't stick together enough to form a dough consistency, add water in drops until the correct consistency is reached careful not to add too much liquid. If you do, add more cacao to balance texture.

3. Scoop out the brownie bite mixture in 1-tablespoon amounts and roll th mixture into balls. Set the balls on the baking sheet and then chill them refrigerator for at least 10 minutes to hold their shape.

4. Transfer the balls to a container with a lid and store in the refrigerator ι ready to eat. You could eat these immediately, but they are more likely t

crumble.

5. Store brownies in an airtight container in the refrigerator for 5 to 7 days

MAKE IT EASIER: Make a double or triple batch of brownies and freeze them. If stored in an airtight container in the freezer, these balls will keep for at least 1 month. Simply pop one out of the freezer when you want a nibble of something sweet.

Per 1-bite serving: Calories: 86; Total fat: 6g; Carbohydrates: 7g; Fiber: 2g; Protein: 3g; Calcium: 14mg; Vitamin D: 0mcg; Vitamin B$_{12}$: 0mcg; Iron: 1mg; Zinc: 1mg

Poached Pears

Serves 4 / Prep time: 10 minutes / Cook time: 20 minutes
GLUTEN-FREE, HIGH-FIBER, ONE-POT, VEGETARIAN

Choosing fruit for dessert over sugar-filled pastries, cakes, and pies is a clear choice if you're looking to cut back on carbohydrates and calories, because whole fruit has more fiber and nutrients. Enjoy these spiced pears, which are poached to tasty perfection.

2 cups white wine, preferably dry

1 cinnamon stick

1 (2-inch) piece of ginger, sliced

5 cardamom pods

Zest and juice of 2 oranges

4 Bosc pears, peeled, cored, and quartered

1. Cut a piece of parchment paper into a circle slightly smaller in size than saucepan you are using, and punch a small hole in its center.

2. In the medium saucepan, stir together the white wine, cinnamon, ginge cardamom, and orange zest and juice on high heat. Bring to just before a lower the heat so the liquid simmers, and add the pears.

3. Place the parchment paper over the pears. (This will keep just enough pressure for the pears to stay beneath the level of the poaching liquid ar allow steam to escape.)

4. Poach the pears for at least 20 minutes. The more time you have, the m flavor they will absorb.

5. Remove the pears from poaching liquid with a slotted spoon. Eat as is o return the poaching liquid (without the pears) to a simmer until the liqu reduces to a syrupy sauce, about 10 minutes. Strain the sauce and pour i the poached pears.

6. Store the pears in an airtight container in the refrigerator for up to 4 day

INGREDIENT TIP: My choice of pear for poaching would be a Bosc pear for both its flavor and ability to hold its shape during the poaching process, although the Anjou, Concorde, and French butter pears are also quite lovely. Avoid Comice and Bartlett pears if you can when making this recipe, as they don't hold up as well.

Per serving: Calories: 228; Total fat: <1g; Carbohydrates: 35g; Fiber: 6g; Protein: 1g; Calcium: 33mg; Vitamin D: 0mcg; Vitamin B_{12}: 0mcg; Iron: 1 mg; Zinc: <1mg

Orange Praline with Yogurt

Serves 6 / Prep time: 10 minutes / Cook time: 10 minutes
GLUTEN-FREE, ONE-POT, VEGETARIAN

We have to thank the French immigrants who settled in Louisiana in the 19th century for introducing praline to the American South. Combine oranges, another staple of Southern desserts, and Greek yogurt as a substitute for cream, and voilà, you have a delicious dessert ready-made for those looking to cut back on carbohydrates.

3 tablespoons sugar

4 teaspoons water

⅓ cup slivered almonds, toasted

½ teaspoon ground cinnamon

⅛ teaspoon ground cloves

1 tablespoon orange zest (optional)

Pinch kosher salt

3 cups plain Greek yogurt

1. Preheat the oven to 375°F. Line a baking sheet with parchment paper.

2. In a small saucepan, stir together the sugar and water and cook over hig until light golden-brown in color, 3 to 4 minutes. Do not stir, but instead gently swirl to help the sugar dissolve. Add the almonds and cook for 1 minute. The goal is to coat the almonds with the heated sugar (think car here) without burning. Pour the mixture onto the prepared baking shee set aside to cool for about 5 minutes.

3. Meanwhile, in a medium bowl, stir together the cinnamon, cloves, oranç (if using), and salt.

4. Break the praline into smaller pieces and toss them in the spices.

5. Evenly divide the yogurt among six bowls and serve topped with the spi praline. Store the praline in a sealed container at room temperature for

2 weeks.

INGREDIENT TIP: The praline can be sprinkled over anything creamy (frozen yogurt) or fruity (grilled peaches or fresh strawberries), so feel free to add it in moderation to your own creations.

Per serving: Calories: 163; Total fat: 8g; Carbohydrates: 12g; Fiber: 1g; Protein: 12g; Calcium: 154mg; Vitamin D: <1mcg; Vitamin B_{12}: <1mcg; Iron: <1mg; Zinc: 1mg

Coconut Macaroons

Makes 12 / Prep time: 10 minutes / Cook time: 20 minutes
VEGETARIAN

Macaroons are an ancient treat traced all the way back to the Italian aristocracy of the 9th century. These cookies remain popular at dinner parties and celebrations today. The balanced flavors of the macaroon are timeless: delicate almond and coconut with a touch of sweetness. Whip up a batch of these treats when you're looking for a delicious dessert that doesn't have as much sugar as some of the more modern choices.

1⅓ cups unsweetened shredded coconut

⅓ cup granulated sugar

2 tablespoons all-purpose flour

⅛ teaspoon kosher salt

2 large egg whites, at room temperature

½ teaspoon almond extract

1. Preheat the oven to 325°F. Line a baking sheet with parchment paper.

2. In a small bowl, stir together the coconut, sugar, flour, and salt until wel combined. Create a well in the center and add the egg whites and almon extract. Mix the two together, then slowly mix the egg white mixture int coconut mixture.

3. Spoon the batter onto the baking sheet in 1-tablespoon amounts, makin about 12 cookies in total. If they aren't rounded, use your hands to gentl each into a ball.

4. Bake the cookies for 18 to 20 minutes, until golden brown. Allow to cool enjoy.

5. Store the cookies at room temperature in an airtight container for up to week.

VARIATION: Coffee or vanilla extract can be used in place of the almond extract. You can also fold in different nuts if you want more of a crunch to the cookie.

Per 1-macaroon serving: Calories: 98; Total fat: 7g; Carbohydrates: 9g; Fiber: 2g; Protein: 2g; Calcium: 7mg; Vitamin D: <1mcg; Vitamin B$_{12}$: <1mcg; Iron: 1mg; Zinc: <1mg

Chocolate Tahini Bombs

Makes 15 each / Prep time: 20 minutes / Cook time: 8 minutes
5-INGREDIENT, GLUTEN-FREE, VEGETARIAN

Sesame is the unsung hero of the dessert world and a healthier way to enjoy something sweet. Tahini, the ground product of toasted sesame seeds, contains more protein than milk and most nuts. This fragrant paste is a rich source of B vitamins, which boost energy and brain function; vitamin E, which helps fight heart disease and stroke; and minerals like magnesium, iron, and calcium. It's amazing to find all of this nutritional power in a simple dessert.

15 whole dates, pits removed (date intact, not split in half completely)

2½ tablespoons tahini, divided

½ cup canned coconut milk

4 ounces dark chocolate, chopped

1 tablespoon toasted sesame seeds

1. Line a baking sheet with parchment paper.

2. Fill each date with a small amount of the tahini, roughly ¼ teaspoon, ar place them on the prepared baking sheet. Put the filled dates in the free: 10 to 15 minutes.

3. Meanwhile, heat the coconut milk in a small saucepan over medium-lov simmering.

4. Place the chocolate in a medium heatproof bowl, and when the milk is simmering, pour it into the bowl and let stand for 3 minutes to soften th chocolate.

5. Stir the mixture until it is smooth and the chocolate is completely melte

6. Remove the dates from the freezer and dip one date at a time into the chocolate. Coat evenly using a fork and place them back on the baking sl Sprinkle the dates with the sesame seeds and repeat until all dates are c in chocolate.

7. Allow to cool completely for the chocolate to harden, or eat immediatel[y]

INGREDIENT TIP: If the chocolate is not melting, do not put it in the microwave! Place the bowl in a saucepan filled with a few inches of gently simmering water over low heat and stir the chocolate until it melts.

Per 1-tahini-bomb serving: Calories: 97; Total fat: 6g; Carbohydrates: 10g; Fiber: 2g; Protein: 1g; Calcium: 20mg; Vitamin D: 0mcg; Vitamin B_{12}: <1mcg; Iron: 1mg; Zinc: <1mg

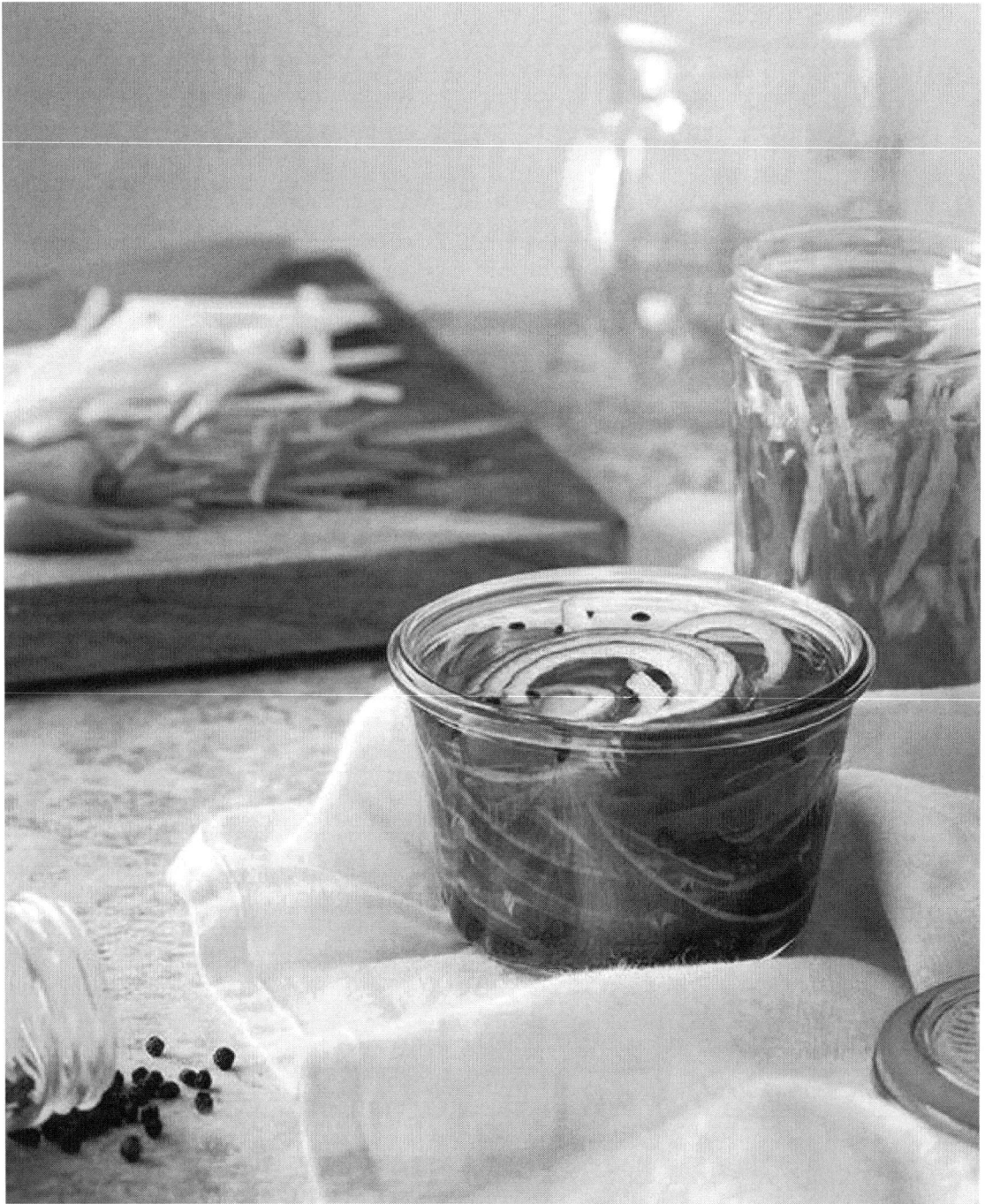

Quick-Pickled Vegetables

CHAPTER NINE
Seasonings, Sauces, and Dressings

This chapter contains all the seasonings, sauces, and dressings that bring out the best in the recipes I've covered in this book. A tasty dish has many components, and it is the relationship between those components—the way each ingredient works with another—that creates perfection on the plate. Over the years, I've enjoyed experimenting and playing around with how tastes work together—for example, what spice blend produces a chorus of unique flavors, how much oil to blend or salt to add to a salad dressing, or what sauce complements a beautiful cut of meat or grain bowl. It is my hope that this chapter not only gives you the tools you need to make my seasonings, sauces, and dressings, but also inspires you to play around with your own ideas. Cooking is a journey after all, and this chapter is here to guide you on the next step.

QN

Lemon Vinaigrette Dressing

Makes 1 cup / Prep time: 5 to 10 minutes
GLUTEN-FREE, NO-COOK, ONE BOWL, VEGETARIAN

Here is a basic lemon vinaigrette recipe that is versatile and super easy to make. In fact, it's so easy, you'll never want to buy it premade again! The fresh lemon juice is key, so be sure to avoid the premade, shelf-stable juice in the grocery aisle. It cannot compete with fresh in this case. Use the vinaigrette as a marinade, drizzle it over roasted vegetables, toss it with a cooked grain, or use it in place of other dressings.

¼ cup freshly squeezed lemon juice

2 garlic cloves, minced

1 teaspoon Dijon mustard

½ teaspoon maple syrup (optional)

¼ cup extra-virgin olive oil

½ cup grapeseed oil

Kosher salt

Freshly ground black pepper

1. In a small bowl, whisk together the lemon juice, garlic, mustard, and ma syrup (if using). Slowly whisk in the extra-virgin olive oil, followed by th grapeseed oil, until the dressing is completely emulsified. Season with s and pepper to taste.

2. Store the dressing in an airtight container for up to 1 week in the refrige or in the freezer for up to 3 months.

INGREDIENT TIP: Grapeseed oil has a neutral flavor, which is why I often combine it with a good-tasting extra-virgin olive oil in my salad dressings. Sometimes extra-virgin olive oil alone can taste grassy, so adding another neutral oil can balance it out. That said, you can replace the grapeseed oil with additional extra-virgin olive oil.

Per 2-tablespoon serving: Calories: 184; Total fat: 20g; Carbohydrates: 1g; Fiber: <1g; Protein: <1g; Calcium: 2mg; Vitamin D: 0mcg; Vitamin B_{12}: 0mcg; Iron: <1mg;

Zinc: <1mg

Chile-Lime Dressing

Makes 1 cup / Prep time: 5 minutes
GLUTEN-FREE, NO-COOK, ONE BOWL

This dressing is so dynamic and flavorful you don't really need much else in your salad. It brings life into the simplest of greens. However, the dressing doesn't need to be limited to salad alone. You can try it on fish, chicken, roasted vegetables, and rice with stellar results.

5 ounces grapeseed or safflower oil

Zest and juice of 4 limes

4 garlic cloves, minced

4-inch piece fresh ginger, minced

2½ tablespoons chile paste

2 teaspoons fish sauce (optional)

¼ teaspoon kosher salt

1. Combine the grapeseed oil, lime zest and juice, garlic, ginger, chile paste sauce (if using), and salt in a jar or container with a tight-fitting lid. Clos lid and shake the mixture vigorously to combine.

2. Store the dressing in an airtight container for up to 1 week in the refrige or in the freezer for up to 3 months.

MAKE IT EASIER: Use the back of a spoon to peel the ginger, and make sure you roll the lime before zesting and juicing. Rolling breaks open the cells that release the juice.

Per 2-tablespoon serving: Calories: 179; Total fat: 18g; Carbohydrates: 6g; Fiber: <1g; Protein: <1g; Calcium: 6mg; Vitamin D: 0mcg; Vitamin B$_{12}$: 0mcg; Iron: <1mg; Zinc: <1mg

Poppy Seed Dressing

Makes 1 cup / Prep time: 5 minutes
GLUTEN-FREE, NO-COOK, ONE POT, VEGETARIAN

There's a sweetness to this dressing that is addictive but also comforting; it reminds me of something my grandmother used to make in her small kitchen in northern Minnesota. But even if you're not from the Midwest, this dressing can conjure up a vision of cozy family dinners. These meals highlight the beauty of cooking and eating together.

½ cup plain Greek yogurt

¼ cup white wine vinegar

3 tablespoons grapeseed oil

2 tablespoons Dijon mustard

1 tablespoon honey

1 small shallot, minced

1½ tablespoons poppy seeds

1. In a blender, puree the yogurt, vinegar, grapeseed oil, mustard, honey, a shallot. Transfer to a container or jar with a lid and stir in the poppy see you don't have a blender, mix by hand in a medium bowl using a whisk o to a jar with a fitted lid and shake vigorously.

2. Store the dressing in an airtight container for up to 1 week in the refrige or in the freezer for up to 3 months.

VARIATION: Use a neutral oil such as canola in place of the grapeseed oil for a different flavor profile.

Per 2-tablespoon serving: Calories: 83; Total fat: 7g; Carbohydrates: 4g; Fiber: 1g; Protein: 2g; Calcium: 44mg; Vitamin D: 0mcg; Vitamin B$_{12}$: <1mcg; Iron: <1mg; Zinc: <1mg

Tahini Dressing

Makes 1 cup / Prep time: 5 minutes
GLUTEN-FREE, NO-COOK, ONE BOWL, VEGETARIAN

Tahini dressing is one of those special ingredients that can be used for almost anything: Dinner? Sure, pour it across anything from steak to chicken or rice to just about any vegetable. Dessert? Well, if you've tried the Chocolate Tahini Bombs, you'll understand its sweeter side as well. I also like to use tahini dressing for breakfast as a topping for fresh greens and a soft-boiled egg on the side.

⅔ cup filtered water

⅓ cup tahini

¼ cup freshly squeezed lemon juice (about 2 lemons)

1 tablespoon extra-virgin olive oil

2 teaspoons maple syrup

Kosher salt

Freshly ground black pepper

1. In a small bowl, whisk together the water, tahini, lemon juice, extra-virg olive oil, and maple syrup. Season to taste with salt and pepper. Adjust t consistency by adding more water or extra-virgin olive oil.

2. Store the dressing in an airtight container for up to 1 week in the refrige or in the freezer for up to 3 months.

VARIATION: Try honey, agave, or even molasses in place of maple syrup. These sweeteners all balance the dressing and add a unique taste.

Per 2-tablespoon serving: Calories: 81; Total fat: 7g; Carbohydrates: 4g; Fiber: 1g; Protein: 2g; Calcium: 45mg; Vitamin D: 0mcg; Vitamin B_{12}: 0mcg; Iron: 1mg; Zinc: <1mg

Caesar Dressing, Two Ways

Makes ~1½ cups of each dressing / Prep time: 5 minutes
GLUTEN-FREE (CHECK WORCESTERSHIRE), NO-COOK, ONE-POT

Caesar salad has made its way into the pantheon of American staples. Very few restaurants, whether a steakhouse, Italian taverna, or grab-and-go joint, omit this dish from the menu. I've developed a couple of different ways to enjoy it here—a classic, lighter version and a vegan version—both of which allow you to enjoy its rich, umami goodness while keeping things focused on health.

For the Classic Light Version

1 cup plain Greek yogurt

¼ cup freshly squeezed lemon juice (about 2 lemons)

4 anchovy fillets, coarsely chopped

2 tablespoons Dijon mustard

2 tablespoons extra-virgin olive oil

3 garlic cloves, peeled

1 teaspoon Worcestershire sauce

Pinch freshly ground black pepper

1. Place the yogurt, lemon juice, anchovies, mustard, extra-virgin olive oil, garlic, Worcestershire, and pepper in a blender and puree until smooth. Adjust the seasonings as desired.

2. Store in an airtight container for 5 to 7 days, or in the freezer for up to 3 months.

For the Vegan Version

½ cup raw sunflower seeds, soaked in water for 2 hours or overnight

¼ cup extra-virgin olive oil

3 tablespoons freshly squeezed lemon juice

2 garlic cloves, minced

1 tablespoon nutritional yeast

1 tablespoon tahini

1 teaspoon Dijon mustard

1 teaspoon maple syrup

½ teaspoon tamari

1. Drain the sunflower seeds and place them in a blender with the extra-vi
   olive oil, lemon juice, garlic, nutritional yeast, tahini, mustard, maple sy
   and tamari. Blend until smooth. If the dressing is too thick, slowly strea
   cold water as the machine is running and blend until smooth. Adjust the
   seasonings as desired.

2. Store in an airtight container in the refrigerator for 5 to 7 days or in the
   freezer for up to 3 months.

MAKE IT EASIER: Both versions of this dressing will keep for at least 1 week if stored in the fridge or for 1 month in the freezer, so double it up to have extra for those times you don't want to cook.

Classic Light Version per 2-tablespoon serving: Calories: 44; Total fat: 3g; Carbohydrates: 2g; Fiber: <1g; Protein: 2g; Calcium: 26mg; Vitamin D: 0mcg; Vitamin B_{12}: <1mcg; Iron: <1mg; Zinc: <1mg

Vegan Version per 2-tablespoon serving: Calories: 87; Total fat: 8g; Carbohydrates: 3g; Fiber: 1g; Protein: 2g; Calcium: 12mg; Vitamin D: 0mcg; Vitamin B_{12}: 1mcg; Iron: 1mg; Zinc: <1mg

Cherry Barbecue Sauce

Makes 2 cups / Prep time: 5 minutes

GLUTEN-FREE, NO-COOK, ONE POT, VEGETARIAN

Is there anything more American than barbecue? It's essential for lazy summer nights with neighbors or family gatherings on the Fourth of July. If you grew up with a grill as a staple cooking method as I did, just the smell of a good barbecue sauce would evoke powerful memories of time spent with people you love. This sweet, tangy cherry barbecue sauce honors these memories while helping create new ones as well.

10 ounces pitted fresh cherries

1 small onion, quartered

2 tablespoons Dijon mustard

2 tablespoons red wine vinegar

1 tablespoon ground fennel seeds

3 chipotle peppers in adobo sauce, plus 1 tablespoon sauce

Pinch freshly ground black pepper

1. In a blender, combine the cherries, onion, mustard, vinegar, fennel, chip peppers, adobo sauce, and black pepper. Puree until combined and adju seasonings as desired.

2. Store in an airtight container in the refrigerator for up to 1 week or in th freezer for up to 3 months.

MAKE IT EASIER: Frozen cherries are an excellent substitute for the fresh ones in this recipe, but you must thaw the fruit beforehand. The best part is that they come pitted, saving you the effort.

Per ¼-cup serving: Calories: 39; Total fat: 1g; Carbohydrates: 8g; Fiber: 2g; Protein: 1g; Calcium: 18mg; Vitamin D: 0mcg; Vitamin B$_{12}$: 0mcg; Iron: <1mg; Zinc: <1mg

Basic Marinara

Makes 8 cups / Prep time: 5 minutes / Cook time: 25 minutes
GLUTEN-FREE, ONE POT, VEGETARIAN

What is left to say about marinara that hasn't already been said? There's a reason why classic pasta and pizza recipes still call for this ode to fresh tomatoes and basil. The beauty of great dishes often lies in their simplicity and balance. In this recipe, I add just enough garlic, oregano, and black pepper to hit the right spot every time.

¼ **cup extra-virgin olive oil**

1 small onion, minced

4 garlic cloves, thinly sliced

2 basil sprigs

1 teaspoon dried oregano

2 (28-ounce) cans diced or crushed tomatoes

Kosher salt

Freshly ground pepper

1. Heat the extra-virgin olive oil in a medium heavy stockpot over medium Cook the onion, stirring occasionally, until very soft, 3 to 5 minutes.

2. Add the garlic and cook, stirring occasionally, until very soft, about 5 mi Add the basil and oregano and stir to combine.

3. Add the tomatoes and bring to a simmer. Reduce the heat to low and sin stirring occasionally, until the sauce is thick, about 15 minutes.

4. Season with salt and pepper.

5. Store in an airtight container in the refrigerator for up to 1 week or in th freezer for up to 3 months.

MAKE IT EASIER: Having extra tomato sauce available is lovely, which is why this recipe makes 8 cups. Store the extra in an airtight container in the freezer if you don't plan to eat all of it within 5 days. Otherwise, you could cut the recipe in half.

Per ½-cup serving: Calories: 59; Total fat: 3g; Carbohydrates: 6g; Fiber: 2g; Protein: 1g; Calcium: 4mg; Vitamin D: 0mcg; Vitamin B$_{12}$: 0mcg; Iron: <1mg; Zinc: <1mg

Tomato, Caper, and Golden Raisin Sauce

Makes ~4 cups / Prep time: 5 minutes / Cook time: 25 minutes
GLUTEN-FREE, ONE-POT, VEGETARIAN

Although this Mediterranean-based sauce is used in the Cauliflower Steaks recipe, it also pairs beautifully with meats like beef, lamb, or chicken and even fish like swordfish and halibut. One could also use it in place of marinara sauce when making pasta for a little more sweetness and an enticing, distinct dish.

2 tablespoons extra-virgin olive oil

6 garlic cloves, minced

1 (28-ounce) can crushed tomatoes

¼ cup golden raisins

2 tablespoons capers

1 teaspoon dried oregano

Pinch kosher salt

Pinch freshly ground black pepper

3 fresh basil leaves

1. Heat the extra-virgin olive oil in a large saucepan over medium heat. Sa the garlic until softened, about 3 minutes. Add the tomatoes, raisins, ca oregano, salt, and pepper and bring the sauce to a simmer. Add the basil leaves, including the stem, and allow them to wilt, then submerge the le in the sauce.

2. Simmer the sauce until thickened, about 15 minutes.

3. Store in an airtight container in the refrigerator for up to 1 week or in th freezer for up to 3 months.

VARIATION: Make the sauce even more exciting with the addition of salty anchovies, olives, or dried herbs such as marjoram, tarragon, parsley, or thyme.

Per ½-cup serving: Calories: 82; Total fat: 4g; Carbohydrates: 12g; Fiber: 2g; Protein: 2g; Calcium: 46mg; Vitamin D: 0mcg; Vitamin B$_{12}$: 0mcg; Iron: 2mg; Zinc: <1mg

Peanut Sauce

Makes 1 to 1¼ cups / Prep time: 5 to 10 minutes
HIGH-FIBER, NO-COOK, ONE BOWL, VEGETARIAN

Peanut butter, and peanuts, in general, have gotten a lot of love over the years. Peanut sauce is used in pan-Asian dishes, especially those developed by Thai and Laotian immigrants and other members of the Southeast Asian diaspora. These exotic dishes prepare peanuts in a way you maybe hadn't seen before. This peanut sauce is a nod to this tradition and works well on everything, such as noodles, chicken, salad, and rice.

½ cup unsalted, unsweetened creamy peanut butter

2 tablespoons soy or tamari sauce

1 tablespoon honey

2 garlic cloves, minced

1 teaspoon diced chile

Juice of 1 lime

1. In a medium bowl, whisk together the peanut butter, soy sauce, honey, g chile, and lime juice until thoroughly combined. Add water to thin out t consistency. Taste and adjust the seasonings as desired.

2. Store in an airtight container in the refrigerator for up to 1 week or in th freezer for up to 3 months.

VARIATION: Add 1 teaspoon of fish sauce or grated ginger if you'd like to try something with more of an umami, or rich and savory, flavor.

Per ¼-cup serving: Calories: 426; Total fat: 34g; Carbohydrates: 20g; Fiber: 6g; Protein: 17g; Calcium: 47mg; Vitamin D: 0mcg; Vitamin B$_{12}$: 0mcg; Iron: 2mg; Zinc: <1mg

Harissa

Makes 2½ cups / Prep time: 15 to 20 minutes / Cook time: 10 minutes
GLUTEN-FREE, VEGETARIAN

Harissa is a North African hot chile pepper paste, the main ingredients of which are roasted red peppers, spices, and herbs. This paste has a kick—it fills your mouth immediately with a bright, fiery flavor. I've toned this recipe down a bit by swapping out the spicier peppers for red bell peppers, although you can still use those hotter ingredients. This does not diminish the quality of the condiment one bit, so it will brighten up your plate.

1 tablespoon coriander seeds

1 tablespoon caraway seeds

4 red bell peppers

4 large garlic cloves

½ cup extra-virgin olive oil

2 teaspoons red pepper flakes

Kosher salt

Freshly ground black pepper

1. In a small skillet over medium-high heat, toast the coriander and caraw
   about 30 seconds. Transfer the mixture to a mortar and pestle or spice
   grinder and grind into powder.

2. Char the bell peppers over a gas flame, in a cast-iron pan, or under the b
   until blackened, about 3 minutes on each side. If using an open flame, r
   and turn each pepper so that the entire pepper chars. Then place the pe
   in a medium bowl, cover the bowl with plastic wrap, and let stand for 5 t
   minutes. When the peppers are cool enough to handle, peel, seed, and p
   them in a food processor. Add the toasted spices, garlic, extra-virgin oli
   and red pepper flakes and pulse to form a uniform paste. Season the har
   with salt and pepper to taste.

3. Store in an airtight container in the refrigerator for 5 to 7 days or in the
   freezer for up to 3 months.

MAKE IT EASIER: Skip the toasting process altogether and use ground spices instead of whole.

Per ¼-cup serving: Calories: 189; Total fat: 19g; Carbohydrates: 7g; Fiber: 3g; Protein: 1g; Calcium: 23mg; Vitamin D: 0mcg; Vitamin B$_{12}$: 0mcg; Iron: 1mg; Zinc: <1mg

Romesco Sauce

Makes ~2 cups / Prep time: 5 to 10 minutes
HIGH-FIBER, NO-COOK, ONE BOWL, VEGETARIAN

Romesco is a tomato-based sauce that comes originally from Catalonia. It might not be quite as well-known as marinara, but it's just as delicious and, in many ways, a bolder culinary ingredient. This recipe will become a go-to favorite with its combination of sherry vinegar, cayenne pepper, paprika, and almond blended with the natural brightness of fresh tomato.

3 roasted red bell peppers

2 slices toasted whole-wheat bread, cubed

1 medium tomato

5 garlic cloves

½ cup toasted almonds

2 tablespoons sherry vinegar

1 tablespoon smoked paprika

¼ teaspoon kosher salt

¼ teaspoon cayenne pepper

¼ cup extra-virgin olive oil

1. In a food processor, combine the bell peppers, bread, tomato, garlic, alm sherry vinegar, paprika, salt, and cayenne. Puree and then, while the ma is running, slowly stream in the extra-virgin olive oil. Stop the machine, and adjust the seasonings as desired.

2. Store in an airtight container in the refrigerator for up to 1 week or in th freezer for up to 3 months.

VARIATION: Swap out the sherry vinegar for others such as cider, white, champagne, or even red wine vinegar.

Per ½-cup serving: Calories: 310; Total fat: 24g; Carbohydrates: 19g; Fiber: 5g; Protein: 8g; Calcium: 101mg; Vitamin D: 0mcg; Vitamin B$_{12}$: 0mcg; Iron: 2mg; Zinc:

1mg

Quick-Pickled Vegetables

Pickles are a great item to keep on hand for many reasons. They are incredibly versatile and can be put on the burger and many other recipes mentioned in this book. You can also use them as a complement to any rice or grain bowl. I like to eat them by themselves after letting the vegetables sit in the brine, because they taste even better the longer they soak. This simple recipe can be stored up to 1 month in the refrigerator, so there's no rush to eat them right away.

Pickled Red Onions

Makes 1½ cups / Prep time: 3 minutes
5-INGREDIENT, GLUTEN-FREE, NO-COOK, ONE BOWL, VEGETARIAN

1 red onion, thinly sliced

1 cup cider vinegar

1 tablespoon whole black peppercorns (optional)

1. In a small bowl, combine the red onion with the cider vinegar and black peppercorns. Allow the onions to marinate for at least 15 minutes and u hour at room temperature.

2. Serve immediately or store in the refrigerator in an airtight container fo to 1 week.

Pickled Carrot and Radish

Makes 2 cups / Prep time: 10 minutes
GLUTEN-FREE, NO-COOK, ONE BOWL, VEGETARIAN

1 cup warm water

2 tablespoons granulated sugar

1 cup carrots, julienne cut or sliced with a peeler

1 cup radish, preferably daikon, julienne cut or sliced with a peeler

1 cup rice wine vinegar

½ teaspoon kosher salt

1. In a small bowl, whisk together the water and sugar. Add the carrots, rac vinegar, and salt. Set aside and allow to marinate for at least 15 minutes up to one hour at room temperature.

2. Serve immediately or store in the refrigerator in an airtight container fc to 1 week.

VARIATION: Adjust the flavor by adding whole spices to either quick pickle. Try fennel seed, dill, mustard seed, or black peppercorns.

Pickled onions per ½-cup serving: Calories: 20; Total fat: <1g; Carbohydrates: 5g; Fiber: 1g; Protein: 1g; Calcium: 12mg; Vitamin D: 0mcg; Vitamin B$_{12}$: 0mcg; Iron: <1mg; Zinc: <1mg

Pickled carrots per ½-cup serving: Calories: 45; Total fat: <1g; Carbohydrates: 11g; Fiber: 2g; Protein: 1g; Calcium: 22mg; Vitamin D: 0mcg; Vitamin B$_{12}$: 0mcg; Iron: <1mg; Zinc: <1mg

Printed in Dunstable, United Kingdom